A RICH DAD LIBRARY

with Foreword by Robert Kiyosaki

HOW TO WIN IN COMMERCIAL REAL ESTATE INVESTING

FIND, EVALUATE & PURCHASE YOUR FIRST COMMERCIAL PROPERTY—IN 9 WEEKS OR LESS

R. CRAIG COPPOLA, CRE, SIOR, CCIM

Published by Rich Dad Library
an imprint of RDA Press, LLC

Any registered trademarks referenced in this book are the property of their respective owners.

RDA Press LLC
15170 N. Hayden Road
Scottsdale, AZ 85260
480-998-5400
Visit our Web sites: RDAPress.com   and   RichDadLibrary.com

Printed in the United States of America

First Edition: January 2014

ISBN: 978-0-991110-40-7

DEDICATION

To all my investors, without whom

I would not have been half as

successful as I am today.

ACKNOWLEDGMENTS

The work of so many people went into this book and the processes outlined within it. Thank you to Kathy Heasley for all her tremendous work and writing. Thank you to all my partners at Lee & Associates and investors who have supported and taught me so much over the years.

CONTENTS

FOREWORD

When you look in a dictionary for the definition of "Professional Real Estate Investor/Broker," Craig Coppola's picture will be there.

As a professional real estate investor for over forty years, I have met many real estate investor/brokers. Craig is the best I have met. He is so good, my wife Kim and I asked him to be our partner on some of our own commercial investments...and they have turned out to be some of the greatest investments we have ever made.

In his book, Craig shares his insights and experiences of the real estate world through his eyes. Craig has not only made Kim and I a lot of money, he has also saved us a lot of money by pointing out nuances we could not see. I am a better investor today because Craig is not only a great commercial real estate investor and broker, he is also a great teacher.

For anyone who wants to do better and become more professional in the world of real estate, this book is priceless.

— Robert Kiyosaki
Rich Dad Poor Dad

CHAPTER 1

WHY COMMERCIAL REAL ESTATE?

When you are in a sales profession, you have the opportunity to win a lot of awards. Funny how those dangling carrots can motivate. I've gone after the carrot many times and have earned six very nice wall plaques inscribed with "Office Broker of the Year." While I'm proud of what these represent—particularly my years of dedicated hard work and relationship building in our industry—they are not where my eyes go every time I walk into my office. No, whenever I walk into my office, I see first a small photo. On it is a piece of land—my first real estate deal that I bought as an investment with investors I put together. That's where my eyes go because it is that photo, that deal, that process that truly excites me.

Commercial real estate is my passion. It moves me every time I see a deal. It makes me anxious when I buy a property. There's the thrill of the hunt. The thrill of the deal. The thrill of the rewards that I don't get anywhere else in my life. My career in commercial real estate keeps me excited and energized for every day and for what it will hold. I live what I like to call "The Real Estate Life." What that means is that I'm one of those people who looks around and doesn't see buildings;

I see opportunities. No matter where I go, I view the world through "real estate eyes," seeing properties with potential along with the countless others I would never touch. Real estate is under my skin.

I didn't get into real estate investing immediately after college. I actually started (and continue today) my real estate career as a commercial real estate broker. It was a good training ground and enabled me to understand what makes one property sell and what keeps others constantly on the market. At that time, my entire livelihood was tied up in real estate and my income was at the mercy of the real estate market's ups and downs. Based on my degree in finance and knowing that a "smart investor" is a diversified investor, I diligently socked away money in various mutual funds and stocks, believing, as most everyone does, that I was building wealth for my future. I believed the statistics that said the stock market, over the long period, delivers an annual rate of return between nine and ten percent. What I didn't know were the subtle details of that statistic. This University of Michigan Study spells it out much better. It reports than an investor who stayed in the U.S. stock market during the entire 30-year period from 1963 to 1993—7,802 trading days—would have had an average annual return of 11.83 percent. However, if the investor missed the 90 best days while trying to time the market, the average return would have fallen to 3.28 percent per annum. That's sobering.

After a few years, I had learned a thing or two about the stock market. The first thing I learned was that it was making me no money. Nearly ten years into my diversification strategy, my investments had hardly appreciated. At the same time, as a commercial real estate broker—and by now a pretty successful one working with big clients—I had been brokering deals that were making the investors, my clients, a lot of money. It was not just a few deals—it was hundreds of deals. I started to see the light. My diversification strategy wasn't working. In fact, it was working against me, and I had no control of the companies I was investing in. That was my second lesson about the stock market: I was putting my future in other people's hands, people I didn't even know and who certainly didn't know me.

Don't get me wrong—at this point I didn't consider myself a real estate investment wizard. I still don't today; there's always something to learn in the ever-changing world of commercial real estate. But I felt sure that if I was handling my own money investing in real estate, I could do better than break-even, as I had been doing with my diversification strategy. I mean, how hard could it be to do better than flat? It was then and there that I made the decision to move beyond commercial real estate brokering and become a real estate investor, too.

THE BIG DECISION

You're probably wrestling with a similar decision right now. You're looking for ways to improve your financial future, and you think real estate might be the answer. Obviously, I believe it is or I wouldn't have written this book. As I look back on my experience, there are many things I'd like to share with you—things that I know now that I wish I had known then, things that would have helped me make the decision to invest much sooner than I did.

Here are some facts:

- There are huge tax advantages to owning real estate that few other investment vehicles can come close to touching.

- Owning real estate is a great investment during inflationary times because, typically, in inflationary periods when prices are rising, so do real estate prices and values.

- There's a freedom that comes with owning real estate because, while it's not a passive investment like a stock, you can make it a semi-passive occupation that affords you free time.

- A large percentage of all the millionaires ever created were in real estate.

- There's a pride of ownership in real estate that you simply don't get when you own stocks.

- You can buy real estate and you can personally help grow your investment.

There are other advantages to owning real estate that you'll learn while reading this book and going through the nine-week program. It took me nearly a decade to discover the advantages and settle on commercial real estate as my primary focus. Through this book, you can benefit from my experience and the wisdom that took me nearly half my career to gain.

YOU CAN BE IN CONTROL

Perhaps you feel the way I did when my money was tied to the stock market. It's like I was on a raft flowing down river with no oars, floating this way and that, into still water sometimes and at other times holding on for dear life heading toward an unknown but promising destination. Not comfortable! I rode the ups; I rode the downs; and I had absolutely no say in where my investments were going. Sure, I got the quarterly performance reports like everyone else, but they were reports of what had happened, not what was going to happen. They were pictures of the past and not actionable today, at least not by me. I felt I had no control.

When I began investing in commercial real estate, I felt actively involved because I was. I was in a boat with oars and I used them, uncovering opportunities, evaluating possibilities, purchasing properties and personally working on their performance. The performance pictures I saw were weekly or monthly, and the numbers told me what I needed to do to improve the results and the value of the property. I was in a position to take action. To me, this was empowering because given my mutual fund managers' performance, I felt confident that I could do better.

That's really the key to being in control: confidence. You simply must believe in yourself and your abilities because everything worth doing takes effort. There will be roadblocks. There will be setbacks. I won't gloss over that, but this book is written to give you confidence by helping you gain knowledge and experience. Trust me, you'll relish the freedom of being in control as much as I do.

REAL ESTATE HAS ITS ADVANTAGES

Aside from the obvious benefits of being in control, real estate offers other advantages. First and foremost, real estate is a hard asset. That means that lenders will loan you money to buy it. In fact, lenders will loan you as much as 75 percent of the purchase price, allowing you to leverage your money and acquire additional properties. On top of that, they will let you borrow against your investment. And at times, you can even get financing that doesn't require a personal guarantee, which means you don't have to risk your home and wealth to invest. Try doing that with stocks!

Perhaps the biggest advantage is that real estate can actually provide you cash flow: monthly cash in your pocket in the form of rent from your investment properties. Aside from a few stocks that pay annual dividends, this "cash flow" is unique to real estate and far surpasses, at least in my experience, any dividend I ever earned through my stock investments. Plus, just try to deduct business expenses from a stock dividend. That's a big "no can do," but you *can* deduct expenses from the rents you collect on your investment properties, and that minimizes your taxes.

Let's talk about appreciation. Real estate appreciates as can stocks, but unlike stocks, you can take the equity out of a property that has increased in value and use it to fund your next investment—tax deferred. If the property has appreciated, you'll have more money to work with as you search for your next investment. Pull the gains out of a stock that has appreciated and you'll be taxed for ongoing or capital gains regardless of whether you reinvest it or splurge on a new car or boat. The IRS treats them both the same: taxable!

Go visit a top-notch tax advisor and he or she will make your head swim with the many tax advantages associated with real estate. I'll keep it simple here because the most lucrative advantage really is simple: the IRS has determined that you can depreciate real estate while it is appreciating in value. So believe it or not, you actually get tax deductions on your investment while it increases in value. There are nuances to this benefit that can even allow you to depreciate certain aspects of your property faster, giving you even bigger tax deductions sooner. This is not a book about the finer points of real estate tax advantages, but I do want to bring the concept of depreciation to the forefront. This is a book written to get you moving and growing in your knowledge and excitement toward your new venture.

Real estate is also an investment you can control. Through your actions you can actually affect the investment's value. For example, you can make sure the property looks nice, you can interact with the tenants, you can do all the things that make your property one that people don't ever want to leave, and improve the return on your investment. Why? Because a commercial property's value is based on its operations and the income that comes from it. Improve operations and income, and you increase the value of the property. But try to improve the operations and increase the income of a company in which you own stock—it's impossible. It's hard to do even when you work for the company! I have a problem with that. I don't like blind faith.

THE ADVANTAGE OF INEFFICIENCY

Allow me to go a little deeper into the concept of advantages. In the investment world, you have two kinds of systems at play: efficient ones and inefficient ones. The stock market is an *efficient* system. Efficient systems are liquid, which means assets can be easily sold for market value. They are immediate, which means valuations are continually assessed and transactions happen instantaneously. They are visible to the masses, meaning everyone has access to the same data, and they create a true "value" at any time because of their instantaneous nature.

Perhaps the best way to define what this all means is through an example. Let's say I own one hundred shares of IBM stock at $100 per share. And let's say IBM has a bad quarter; they miss their earnings estimates by 10 cents and their stock loses $5 per share in value. Not only did my shares lose value, but everyone who owns IBM stock lost share value too. That is how an efficient system works. There are systems and mechanisms in place to ensure that everyone is treated equally. It is very hard to get the unfair advantage in the stock market. You can get it, but it's usually called insider trading and can land you in jail.

Contrast that with real estate, which is an *inefficient* system. It possesses traits that are the exact opposite of the efficient stock market. First, many factors can change when it comes to real estate and those factors can vary by country, region, state, town, and even neighborhood. They include financing, location modifications, multiple uses, zoning changes, multiple tenants in multiple industries, market cycles, functional uses, and more. Even though the word *inefficient* may sound like a negative, it's really a positive ... a big positive. Let's say instead of stock, I invested in a 3,000-square-foot office building in Phoenix that cost me $1 million. News hits that General Motors misses its earnings projections and they are downgrading future sales projections for the rest of the year. Well, of course the General Motors stock will go down on that news and it doesn't matter where I live; if I own the stock, I am hit. But the investment I own in real estate is in the Southwestern U.S. and it houses a business that has nothing to do with the automotive industry. The bad news in Michigan doesn't affect my building or me. However, my friend in Detroit owns a similar building with a tenant that serves the auto industry. My friend is at risk. That's an inefficient system. Business news, trends, the economy hit everyone differently—that holds true in times of declines and in times of upturns. You'd never see stocks behave that way. The point of all this is that when you do your research, you will know your exposures to the market as a whole and will have the unfair advantage. What is called insider trading in stocks is called being smart in real estate, and I love that.

My Revised Investment Allocation Strategy

For ten years, my investment allocation strategy looked like everyone else's and I was not in control, even though I thought I was for a while. Perhaps you've seen, or are investing based on, those typical pie charts that show, according to your age and retirement goals, how much of your investment dollars are in stocks, how much are in bonds, how much in long- and short-term investments, cash or liquid investments. I was among the masses—thanks to my own ignorance and blind faith in the system—investing with the pack in the same places the pack invests. My investment allocation pie chart looked like the next guy's, and the next guy's, and the next.

Yet, I was hoping for better results than what the pack typically gets. That's just crazy. If you invest with the pack, you're going to get the same results as the pack. In every aspect of my life, I had always wanted the unfair advantage. Why was I settling for less here? Now, I've never been willing to do anything underhanded to get an unfair advantage, but I've always been absolutely willing to work harder and smarter to get it. When it became clear that my stock and bond investments gave me no edge, I made some changes. As a result, my new asset allocation looks far different than the pack's. And best of all, it also performs far differently than the pack's.

My revised allocation strategy has delivered more than 23 percent return annually in the last 20 years. It has been through three big real estate cycles—the ups and the downs—and has been actively managed to deliver the results and achieve the goals I've set for it. It wasn't magic. It was about being in control. It was about betting on myself.

I know you can do what I did. I wasn't a financial wizard before I got into this. I was a college graduate learning a new business and a soon-to-be husband. I was pretty much just like you with the desire to not work hard all my life. I didn't come from money and I didn't have a windfall that helped me buy my first property. I was, and am, a regular guy who learned the business and took action.

NOW IS THE TIME

I took action, and that pretty much might be the difference between me and the many other "regular guys." Too often, people say they are going to do things and then they don't do them. Through the many successful people I know, the books I have read, and my own experience, I know that winning takes knowledge, understanding and, most of all, action. If you don't take action, all the knowledge and understanding is just folly. It's action that turns your wants and desires—even your visions of the future—into reality.

Action can make you uncomfortable. It often means change; it takes commitment; and it can involve failure. I should know. Action has taken me further in business, in investing, and in life than I could have imagined. However, it has also brought me failure as well— investments that didn't pan out as well as I thought they would, deals that would not close. Through these trials came learning. Without the actions, I would not have had the learning. I also would not have had the successes: Broker of the Year awards, top producer accolades, and numerous real estate investments that generate income for me and for my investors.

What it comes down to is simply this: success is less about *thinking* and more about *doing*. Included in this book is a program that, if you start today and take action right now, will position you to make your first offer on a property in nine weeks. Even if you say, "I won't be ready to make an offer in nine weeks," read this book and do what it says to do as if you are ready. By the end, you may surprise yourself. At the very least, you will have learned the market and established a network within it. You will be in a better position when you are ready to move forward with your real estate investment career.

I read an article by Dirk Zeller, a well-known real estate agent coach, and in it was something that has stuck with me for years. Zeller said there are two types of pain: the pain of discipline and the pain of regret. I believe what he meant was that, yes, it's hard to get started with something new like real estate investing. It might even be hard to fit this new endeavor into your already-busy schedule. That's the pain of discipline and it is immediate. The pain of regret, however, we can hide from for years, even decades. But when the "could haves" and the "should haves" hit us head on, they are longer-lasting, farther-reaching and very difficult to overcome. I choose the pain of discipline every time. It's immediate, but that's all it is. Even though getting started is not much fun, the feeling of short-term accomplishment is great and the long-term results are often glorious.

CHAPTER 2

TOOLS OF THE TRADE

Every trade has its tools. Of course, it's natural to think of tools in the conventional sense like hammers and saws, computers and phones, maps and charts. Tools come in many forms. I had the honor and the thrill a few years back of being the head coach of our area's Little League All Stars. Being a baseball lover, it was a dream come true because it gave me a chance to really bring these talented kids to the next level in their baseball careers—even if those careers never go much further than high school. Excellent tools were a part of my coaching strategy.

People who know me know I can't do anything in moderation, so when it came to coaching, I approached it in much the same way I've approached everything else I've set out to do in life: with a startling amount of research, analysis, planning, and detail, all in preparation for intense action. I was not coaching a pro team, but that didn't matter. I had batting line ups (based on who from the opposing team was pitching), training schedules, practice schedules, scouting reports, game strategies, substitution plans, even who was going to coach first base. Some of the parents, I'm sure, thought I was going a little overboard.

But to me, "going overboard" was simply preparing the team to face every challenge in practice so that when those same situations came up in a game, they weren't new. That was my job as coach. It was about developing and using the tools that would make the kids and me more effective, and in turn make the team more effective. In essence, my role was to put those kids in a position to win. Sure, the tools were the best bats, balls, gloves, and all those tangible things. The tools were also the intangibles like knowing what to do in a first-and-third situation and in bunt defense, knowing what relays to make, and how to handle a "run down." Those terms may sound obscure to some of you, just as some of the language of real estate might sound to you now. Rest assured, as you read this book, even the most arcane terms and concepts will become part of your vocabulary and part of your tool set.

Baseball and commercial real estate investing aren't all that different. Just like in baseball, commercial real estate investing requires tangible tools that you can hold in your hand and see with your eyes along with intangible ones, like the instincts that come only from preparations, repetition, and experience. In this chapter, I will share with you my most valuable real estate investment tools and how I use them. I highly recommend you get familiar with each of them as you make your way through this nine-week program. They will save you time, frustration and make you more effective in the long run, just like our Little League All Stars who made it all the way to the state finals. We were state runner-ups—that was victory to us. Sixteen wins and three losses on the way to the state finals. They played great and came away a better team and more confident kids. I want the same for you when it comes to commercial real estate investing. I want you to win!

Armed and Effective—The Tangible Tools

Have you ever tried to repair a door that is sticking without the right tools? I have. It's maddening. It's what drives me to pick up the phone whenever we need home repairs. Not only is fixing things something I'm not very good at—I really don't have the right tools—which only enhances how "not good" I am. I hire out *all* home repairs.

When it comes to real estate investing, the opposite is true. I have all the tools. I know how and when to use them and I have gotten good at it over the years. Practice in real estate, like in baseball and door repair, may not make you perfect, but it will sharpen your instincts and your effectiveness. You still need the right tools, and I have found several that are absolutely indispensable to me as I look for property, analyze it, and ultimately quantify its potential. Here's my list of tangible must-haves:

HP12C or HP17B Calculator (or Similar Mobile Apps): Hewlett Packard got it right when it developed these classic 120-function calculators. They truly are designed for financial professionals and come with the ability to calculate the price of a property based on the capitalization rate, amortization, monthly payments, cash flow analysis, net present value, internal rate of return, and more, very quickly and easily. By the way, don't worry about what all those words mean right now; that will come later. Just know that with these calculators, you won't have to actually perform the mathematics behind these calculations.

Mobile smart phone users can do a quick search of financial calculators and find a large number of apps that emulate the HP calculators. MathU 12D Financial Calculator is just one—but they are all inexpensive and worth trying until you find one you like. I now have my HP 12C loaded on my iPad and that works great. You still will need to know how to use this tool and for that, I recommend two helpful handbooks: *The Real Estate Applications Handbook* and the *Leasing Applications Handbook*.

Take time to review these, but also invest in yourself by taking a three-hour class that many real estate schools offer to teach you how to use this powerful tool to do the calculations needed for this business. They will save you tons of time; even if you're the most skilled spreadsheet user. These calculators will allow you to very quickly draw important conclusions about a property no matter where you are, without spending a lot of time. If you prefer to learn through the Internet, HP offers free online videos on demand for its calculators. There are other sources of tutorials available online as well.

You will notice throughout this book, the concept of *simple* wins every time with me. I need to clearly understand in my mind why I like the deal. I never buy a deal I cannot understand in a five-minute conversation. Clear, focused, simple: that is what I am looking for in a real estate deal. In sales, they call it an "elevator pitch." If someone on the twelfth floor asked you what you did for a living and you have only the elevator ride to the ground floor to tell him, what would you say? I do an "elevator pitch" on all my properties. Clear, focused, simple. These calculators and knowing how to use them, help to get me there.

Demographic Data: One of the best tools is a simple one. It's a file —on your computer, in a drawer or in a binder—that contains all the demographics of your city, town, and state. You'll want to know this material inside and out. Demographic data comes in many forms, and at times it will be your best friend because it will reveal to you trends and projections for various areas of your city or town.

The first type of demographic is what I call *micro data* and it's all about drilling down on your area of investment opportunity. I am a big believer in "farming" an area, and farming is nothing more than selecting a small part of your city or town and becoming an expert on it. You farm the plot (area) getting to know it, watching over it, cultivating it, and growing it. The first set of demographics will help you to know what to plant (buy). Is it a fast growing area of town or is it mature? Is the state a Sunbelt state or is it in the Rustbelt? These answers will direct you to the types of investments you will want to buy.

For example, it is easy to buy in Arizona where I live. The region is growing and new developments are everywhere. What about in a more mature market, a market where growth is slow or declining? This is where you look for areas that are the best locations or where there is a resurgence happening. I was in Pittsburgh, Pennsylvania several years back and witnessed this very thing. The city had completely transformed itself. Knowing where other resurgence areas are, which areas are growing, and which are declining, is key to your real estate investment career. It all starts with doing your homework through area demographics.

Knowing where an area currently is, isn't enough. Demographics can help you discover something perhaps more important. Demographics can help you understand the long-term projections of various areas of your town. I think in terms of neighborhoods and blocks rather than zip codes. Every city has them. In New York, it's Greenwich Village and Soho, for example. In the Phoenix metro area, it's the Camelback Corridor and Old Town Scottsdale, to name just a few. Later we'll go over where you find this kind information, but a good start are websites such as Loopnet.com and CoStar.com, which give you a general picture of demographics along with tons of information about specific properties. You can take all this information with you with LoopNet apps for phones and iPads and CoStarGo for the iPad.

Once you begin to visit these sites and use these apps, you'll be tempted to spend hours looking at properties, pricing, and features. Hold that enthusiasm because before you get excited about the building, it's more important to understand where a neighborhood is going. Is it trending up, staying flat, or declining? It's all about looking forward, not backward, because when you're buying real estate, you're buying futures. You must understand why the investment makes sense years from now, not just for today. Let me give you an example. Would you buy a retail building housing a Sizzler Steakhouse in a neighborhood that you knew was trending downhill, where the average household income was $50,000 five years ago and is $35,000 today? Probably not. Because you know the Sizzler wouldn't be there for long in a declining neighborhood. There just would not be enough of the right business and eventually you'd lose your tenant. That's the kind of insight demographics can give you. In this same neighborhood with these demographic trends, you might be interested in a Dollar Store investment.

Maps: It used to be that a map was a map. But thanks to satellite imaging, a map is actually a picture of your town, your block, your street, even your building. The precision in the aerial mapping of many regions of the country is photographic quality. It comes in handy when understanding things like property accessibility, amenities, building density, neighborhood, proximity to other amenities, location feel, and traffic flow. I use maps to get a bird's eye and a street view of a property, the block, and the surroundings, and to validate if what I think to be true really is. And using Google Maps, Google Earth, or another mobile app— tools I take with me when I tour—I jot notes on the various neighborhoods. I have used Google Earth to not only give me the lay of the real estate land, but to even check the accessibility of mountain passes while backpacking in the Sierra Nevada. Just as I can see the quantity of snow and how hard my climb is going to be on a hike, I can count a building's parking spaces and see how accessible a building is from the street. These photographic maps have made my real estate life and my sporting life easier, and in the process made me infinitely smarter. They will do the same for you.

I also use maps to see the characteristics of the surrounding neighborhoods. Maps today have everything. Heck in my car, my GPS shows banks, restaurants, and gas stations as I am driving down the road. Wow!

The Internet: This is an obvious tool because everything we've talked about so far is Internet based. But beyond the obvious, the Internet is the place to go for other important information. As you'll learn later in this book, the tenants within a building are extremely important. Knowing everything you can about their businesses—their profitability, their credit rating, their financials, their clientele, their site requirements, etc.—can help you make good judgments about a building you're considering.

Remember Sizzler Steakhouse? How did I know that a neighborhood with a $50,000 household income average was acceptable and anything below that wasn't? Because a quick search of Sizzler Steakhouse franchising reveals its site selection criteria. The company's many location requirements included a neighborhood with household income no lower than $50,000. It's that easy.

All kinds of tenant information are online which will help you make good property decisions. You'll find investor information, too, which will help you make better partnership decisions. You can look up potential partners and discover if they've had any negative press, legal trouble, or bad business dealings. One time, my assistant did a search on a potential investor in one of my partnerships. She uncovered a $10 million lawsuit filed against him. Good thing she found this nugget! Any money he would have given us could have been tied up in a legal battle for years. I check everything, and the Internet—including social media sites like Facebook, LinkedIn, Twitter, etc.—is the best place to start.

Software: Yes, of course you'll need support from Microsoft. Excel and all the other Microsoft Office programs will come in handy. From developing spreadsheets in Excel, to developing correspondence and proposals in Word, to even developing presentations to obtain financing in PowerPoint, you'll want to get computer savvy as quickly as you can, if you aren't already. Another software application that I use is ARGUS (argussoftware. com), which is an investment analysis program. It is the industry standard for analyzing a property's cash flow, creating "what-if" analyses, determining property valuations, performing sensitivity analysis, and the like. Without ARGUS, you must build your own spreadsheets in Excel. It's certainly possible, but it makes the work much more difficult. CoStar.com, which I mentioned earlier as a place to go for project data, has a database for most major cities and towns that shows every building, how much space is available, if the building is for sale, and the listed price. You must subscribe to this service, but once you do, you can do all your market studies from this one web-based service. Loopnet.com, also mentioned earlier as a source, offers a database that lists all the properties for sale worldwide, much like CoStar.com.

On the property management side the name to know is Yardi (yardi.com), both online and in the mobile app space. I use Yardi to manage things like accounts receivable and accounts payable, leasing, square footage tracking, expenses and rent adjustments. I use all this information along with options to view and print valuable reports. You don't necessarily need Yardi for all the buildings you buy, but should you decide to sell the building eventually, it's actually a valuable selling point to have all your management details on Yardi. Yardi is a program you "grow" into. You do not need it as you buy, but as you grow your portfolio, you can use it to be more sophisticated. Their free mobile apps are a good way to get familiar with the power of all things Yardi.

Capital: This is a tool we all can use, and not just for our budding commercial real estate investment business, but for everything else too. Capital is a requirement for investing—that goes without saying—but specifically, you want to make sure you have some of your own capital to invest. The reason I say this is because in my experience, investors—whether they take the form of banks, institutions, or private individuals—want to know you have money on the line, too. So even if you are planning to raise capital to fund your first property, have at least five to ten percent of the money you expect to raise be your own.

My first investment was small and funded with just four friends. It was not commercial real estate, it was land. We purchased three residential lots in a master-planned development called Mirabel in Scottsdale, Arizona, and I funded a portion of the deal with my own money. Within three years, we closed it out and doubled everyone's money on the asset appreciation. It was a good investment to be sure, but also a good learning experience. Even friends, I found, wanted to make sure I had skin in the game. I haven't met many investors who don't. And that's fine by me. Having your own money in a deal makes it real. It proves to investors that you believe in your own project.

I know it's easy for me to say you need to have some of your own capital in a deal. Maybe right now you don't have the cash. Let me make this simple. If this is your passion, it's time to figure out a way to save some money. Live below your means. Figure out a way to save, borrow, or collateralize an asset to get access to some money. How powerful is it when you go to potential investors on your first deal and say, "I have saved $5,000 over the past two years, putting away only $200/month, just so I could put ALL of it in this deal?" That's commitment. That's passion.

The most important word about capital is this: your real estate capital fund, meaning the dollars you have to invest, should not be the first and only investment/savings you have. People who have no other form of savings and then put everything they have in real estate are rolling the dice. Even though this book will teach you how to minimize the risk involved in real estate, nothing is 100 percent guaranteed. Smart investors have other investment and savings vehicles (some where the principle is guaranteed) before they invest in real estate. Later, you'll see my own asset allocation strategy and understand more fully the reasons behind my thinking.

ARMED AND DANGEROUS—THE INTANGIBLES

Why armed and dangerous? Because anyone can acquire the tools in the preceding section of this chapter, but it's the intangibles that will really make you a force to be reckoned with in your city or town. It's the intangibles that will make you the most money. The hard part is that you can't walk into a store and purchase these tools, you can't log onto the Internet, download an app, and you can't simply attend a training class and walk out an expert. These tools take an investment of your time and your talents. They take commitment and dedication. They take a drive to be the best. Are you ready? Of course you are.

Your Homework: Think back to high school algebra. Unless you were one of those kids who just "got it" the minute the teacher presented a concept, doing the nightly homework—problem after problem, solving for x, then solving for y, over and over—actually helped you understand the concepts, the rules, and the processes. I know it helped me. It also made me more confident in class, and actually more highly regarded by my teacher and, most importantly, with my buddies. We were all competitive with each other, even in math class.

Doing your homework when it comes to your new commercial real estate investing business will do exactly the same thing. You'll learn the concepts, rules, and processes along with all the particulars of your market. You'll gain confidence and you'll be taken more seriously by the professionals in the industry and with investors. Today, those buddies who drove me to do better in algebra *are* my investors. And today they drive me to do my real estate homework, no matter how much I think I know. If you want to be taken seriously in this business and be successful, doing your homework is more than a must. It's a critical prerequisite for establishing a solid reputation. Reputation leads to contacts, and like in every business, in real estate investing, contacts are golden.

Experience: Granted, this is one tool you won't have right when you start, but it is one tool that you will have the power to acquire quickly. In fact, you will walk away from your first commercial real estate deal knowing more than you can possibly imagine right now. And, at the same time, if you're like me, you'll walk away, wishing you had known more.

My first commercial real estate deal can be better described as my first "potential" real estate deal. I say potential because it was a 12,000-square-foot multi-tenant office building in Phoenix. At the time I was looking at it, it was fully leased. It looked like a great investment opportunity, and I was excited to be well on my way to owning my first commercial property. I had the investor lined up, but had to do all the due diligence with money out of my own pocket to make sure it was the right deal. Everything checked out great, except for one thing. During the roof inspection, my contractor noticed some holes in the parapet on the roof. He found they were leaking water down the inside walls of the building. This is never good because water within walls can cause a lot of damage, including wood rot and mold. The risks of incurring major repairs were too great, so rather than close, I walked away from the deal with a loss of $15,000 of my own due diligence money. It was a tough decision, but it was the right one. That experience helped me learn that there are many ways a deal can fall apart and that you have to check them all. It showed me what I needed to know next time around—the homework that I will always do. It showed me the right way to work with an investor. He was grateful for my decision and it only increased his confidence in me. He is now one of my repeat investors. Why? Because he saw that I would always do the right thing even if it cost me money, and for that reason he trusts me.

I also learned a good lesson about how I define a good deal. After my $15,000 lesson, I began looking for deals that had bigger margins so that if walls needed repair, I could contract the work and still have a solid cushion. Margin became my mantra after that because unexpected things happen and it takes deals with a margin to survive. As you can see, there were a lot of lessons in that $15,000 price tag. Lessons that have probably saved me millions. The whole experience, of course, was painful, but it made me a better business person, a better partner, and a whole lot wiser for the next time.

People: Can people really be tools? Let's not mess with semantics, but if tools are helpful, then people are tools because people have been helping me succeed my entire career. I wouldn't be anywhere without the tremendous people I have met along the way. They've taught me everything—not always the easy way—but their lessons were mine for the taking.

I have a savvy investor client. When I want to get a piece of information on trends from a global perspective, I go to him. He has been in the game a long time and I really respect his guidance and advice. Getting advice from seasoned veterans is sometimes enlightening, sometimes reassuring, but always thought-provoking. Sometimes it makes you mad, too.

People were also responsible for giving me early breaks and important opportunities. Another important influence and a person to whom I give much of the credit for my real estate career is Charley Freericks, a guy I met in college. While I was focusing on playing baseball, he had secured a position with a very successful brokerage company in Arizona. It was through him that I got a meeting with his boss and eventually a job with his boss's brother's company. In my new position, I learned everything I could, and within eighteen months, my new-found contacts helped me get my first job with the same prominent commercial real estate brokerage company Charley worked for. Six years later, it was these same folks who saw the value in me, along with several others who launched Lee & Associates Arizona, the firm I still work with to this day. It's an excellent firm, and my position within it has allowed me to grow and to discover just how small the world of commercial real estate really is and how we all help each other. Today, I'm thrilled to help others in the field—that's the primary motivation for writing this book. I tell you this story to prove that people and the relationships you have with them are everything. People not only help you find your next career breaks, they can be valuable sources of information that don't make it into any directory or onto an Internet site. That leads to my final point about how the "people" tool works. You are "people," too, and as such, you'll be a tool for someone else. Sooner than you think, you'll have information and knowledge to share. Don't be shy. Reciprocal relationships are generally the best and most lasting kind.

Growth Market: If you're in a growth market, meaning a town or city that is growing, then you are in a great place to be. A growth market is a "nice-to-have" tool, but not a required one. So if you aren't in a high-growth market, don't worry, there are still plenty of opportunities. You just have to buy right. As you begin looking at your town or city with "real estate eyes"—meaning you don't just see streets and buildings, you see opportunities— you'll find plenty of plums that are ripe for the taking. People in every city and every town are making money on real estate— or, if they don't invest wisely, losing it. I want to put you in the first camp. A large portion of the nine-week plan is dedicated to doing that: minimizing risks by making you smarter through knowledge, people, and processes.

A Feel for the Business: How do you get a feel for the business? Well, think about the business you are currently in. If you've been doing it for a while, you likely have a feel for the business. You may not even realize it until a new person arrives on the scene and you are startled by how much you know and can instinctively do, by comparison. In commercial real estate, like in any business, getting a feel for it takes time and getting your hands dirty. By that I mean it takes getting deeply connected into the commercial real estate network in your town. It takes reading everything you can on the subject. And most importantly, it takes big action and small action.

There's a short video and a simple book that I love. It's called *212 Degrees* by S.L. Parker. Among the many important lessons from this book, which focuses on the fact that it takes just one degree to make water go from hot to boiling, is that a tiny amount of extra effort makes all the difference. Put into non-metaphorical terms, Parker also quotes Earl Nightingale and states that if you spend one extra hour a day on your chosen profession, within five years you will be an expert.

I believe it. The difference between good and great is inches, not miles. *National Geographic* photographer, Dewitt Jones, demonstrates that point through his photography as he speaks to audiences around the world. He spoke at a conference I attended and showed through his amazing photography that the difference between a "good shot" and a "great shot" is often miniscule from the camera's perspective but monumental from the eye's perspective. To me, Jones and Parker both show that becoming proficient takes big action, but becoming an expert takes small action—that extra effort that separates the good from the great.

I don't just believe in this, I practice it. I have developed and use a select training program called a Runner Program for turning ordinary people into commercial real estate brokers. Call it paying their dues, but really, it's designed to make them turn into experts. It goes like this: they work for normal money and put in long hours (a minimum of 80 hours a week) for three years. The first six months, they do not get to meet a client, see a deal, or step outside. It's a little like boot camp. But it's required. What do they do? They make copies; make maps; learn how to research properties; and learn all our systems, programs, etc. When they finally get out, they *know,* really know, all the backstage functions of the business. They can do it even in their sleep and never have to think about that part of the business again. As you can imagine, many don't cut it; they don't believe in themselves or want it enough. But the ones who do become very successful.

Belief: Without getting too philosophical here, believing you can do all this—all the research, the learning, the action—is a prerequisite for your success. That applies not just to commercial real estate, but to anything else you want to do in life. As I began my real estate career, I wanted to stay physically active, so I took up distance running. I had never done it before, but as I got into it, I found it motivating and empowering. I ran a bunch of marathons, then I decided to set my sites on ultra-running events (ultra-running is any event longer than a marathon) culminating with the Marathon des Sables (www.marathondessables.com).

If you have not yet heard of this event, it is an annual 152-mile, seven-day, self-supported stage race in 130-degree heat in the Sahara Desert. I could not have completed it without the belief that I could do it. Runners got nine liters of water per day, and the rest of our food and gear we had to carry ourselves. We got a flare gun in case of emergency, which I came close to using. The difference between hydrated and dehydrated is a matter of minutes in the Sahara for humans. At one point in the race, we spotted a casbah village and finished our water about seven minutes before getting to it. When we got there, we were parched and discovered it wasn't a water station at all. Knowing we were in trouble, we continued on to the crest of the hill, and spotted a water station off in the distance. By the time we got to it, we were dehydrated. My buddy was so dehydrated that he ended the race with an IV in his arm, lying under a Land Rover. It took all the belief I could muster after that to finish this race. That day's remaining fifty miles were the loneliest I've ever run. Many times I heard that voice that said, "Stop now! Are you crazy?" But I had the belief. I knew I could finish, and I did.

Real Estate investing is like running marathons. You'll have those voices in your head, too, as you embark up on the trek to becoming a real estate investor. Luckily, dehydration won't be a problem, but along the way, belief probably will be. Expect it and move beyond it, just as I did in the race. By the next day, with my buddy out of the race, I began running with a few new people who gave me the strength I needed to continue. "I have trained for this. I can finish," I thought, and with their companionship and our mutual encouragement, we all went on to not only complete the race, but clock a respectable finish. Find the belief within yourself and surround yourself with others who believe in you, too.

From this point forward, we'll focus on the actual nine-week process. The reasons why you'll need to buy that calculator, why you'll want your computer all set up with the right software and a high speed Internet connection, and why you'll need to gather as much research materials about your market as you can will become clearer soon. You'll also learn exactly what the nature of the "homework" is and you'll see exactly who the "people" are who will become your greatest asset … and you, theirs. You'll also understand why believing in yourself is perhaps the best tool of all.

CHAPTER 3

THE NINE-WEEK PROCESS

My kids are all school age and because of them, I'm reminded four times a year how long nine weeks actually is. They are quick to tell me that nine weeks is the length from the beginning to the end of the typical school term. I remember it well, myself. On day one, we'd cover our school books, and on the final day of the term, we'd take home our report card with glee, with fear, or something in between. Those nine weeks used to feel like forever. Funny how, as we age, nine weeks go by so quickly. It's almost scary.

Well, these nine weeks to making an offer will go by extremely fast, too. You'll be busy doing the work of a real estate professional, and you'll most likely be holding down your day job, that is, the work you're doing right now and from which you may hope to be free very soon. These nine weeks will be no different from any other goal—like training for a marathon or working to slim down before that 20-year class reunion. It will take drive, energy, and consistency, but in nine weeks, just like consistent exercise can transform your body, performing the tasks in this book can transform your life and your wealth outlook.

I've never been a person who wavered much once I put my mind to something. The same was true when I started investing in the stock market. I was going for it. It was the right thing to do and I was going to stick with it. It was Christmas 1988 and my sister-in-law gave me Robert Kiyosaki's *Rich Dad Poor Dad*. I thanked her and read it within a week. Thoroughly impressed, I suggested that a friend of mine who was in the midst of a career change take a look at it. He loved it, too, and headed down to the bookstore where Robert Kiyosaki was doing a book signing. He bought ten more books and told Robert my story. Within a few days, I got a call from Robert himself, and we decided to meet for breakfast. He drew a diagram on a napkin of what later became the CASHFLOW Quadrant®. To learn more about it, read Robert's book, *CASHFLOW Quadrant*. It will change your life if it hasn't already. That's when the light bulb went off for me, and I realized that my current investment strategy was something I simply had to quit. Quitting anything is hard for me, but this book was the kick in the pants that I needed. It was time to invest in myself. You most likely are there, too, since you're reading this book.

The process of becoming a commercial real estate investor is an ongoing one that has taken me more than twenty years to hone, and I continue to develop my skills and abilities every day. I didn't start out knowing this stuff, believe me. I made, and still make, my share of mistakes. I have lost money and still lose money. I continue to learn with every deal. That's the payoff of mistakes. They are worth the price if they make you wiser. You'll make mistakes, too. The information in this book, when followed, will minimize them. So let's get to an overview of the nine weeks that can change your life.

WEEK 1

FOCUS YOUR GOALS

You've heard it before, the whole idea of goal setting, and here it is again. There's no getting around it. You have to know where you want to go to get there. For some of you, this will be easy. For others, coming to terms with your goals will be challenging. So in the first week, your mission is to get to know your own wants and needs. These are some of the specifics you'll need to consider: What is my financial position and how much can I afford to invest? What kind of commercial real estate interests me? Am I looking for a building for my business, and if so, what are my needs? Can I invest alone, or will I need investors? In other words, develop the clearest vision of what you want at the end of nine weeks. Even if you think you already know what you want, follow the program and go through the exercise of self-evaluation and reflection. Write everything down. You may be surprised at the outcome. You may go in with clarity only to find that the more you investigate and think about it, things aren't quite so clear. You may end up with a goal that is quite different from one you originally thought you had.

WEEK 2

LEARN YOUR LOCAL REAL ESTATE LANDSCAPE

Whenever I talk to people new to real estate investing, they often say they don't care what kind of product type they invest in, they just want to make money. I can appreciate that; I felt the same way initially. Then I learned better. Ultimately, you do care; you just don't know it yet. I didn't either when I first started out. What you'll find is that it's really hard, pretty much impossible, to master every type of commercial product out there. There are simply too many nuances, and just too much to know with each of them. I haven't even begun to talk about the work involved in keeping current with the market for every commercial product type. It's just beyond the scope of any one person. Narrowing is an imperative.

This is the first week that you'll go outside of yourself and start taking in the real estate world. It's your first venture into the community looking through "real estate eyes," where buildings aren't buildings, they're opportunities. You'll drive around and you'll get to know your city or town in a whole new way. There will be parts of it you'll like and other parts you won't. Eventually, you'll get a feeling for what is right for you.

Absolutely at this stage, some of your decisions will be based on gut. That's good because at this point, your gut is your most reliable indicator. My gut told me I liked business and being in the business world, so commercial office space was a natural product type choice for me. But I didn't know that on day one. It took time.

There's a Chinese proverb that fits here. It says, "Before enlightenment, chop wood and carry water. After enlightenment, chop wood and carry water." Of course, you may interpret this in many ways, but to me this proverb says that through enlightenment you may arrive at the same conclusion you had in the first place, but you'll understand its meaning.

I felt that way when I began my career in commercial real estate. Having been a broker for a number of years, I felt I had a handle on the market. I knew where the opportunities were. But after setting my first goal, and really deciding my love was commercial office space, I noticed that my "favorite" part of town as a broker wasn't necessarily my favorite as an investor. Opportunities now are in many parts of the city—as an investor. I'm still chopping wood and carrying water, I just understand why I'm doing it, where I'm doing it, and for what purpose.

What you'll find is that, at this stage, you simply must narrow down locations to one or two. I'll show you how to do this and then what to do once you've made your choice. Just as it is impossible to focus on every commercial product type, there's no way that any single person, no matter how small the city in which he or she lives, can focus on every part of the city. In case you haven't caught on by now, the first two weeks are a process of narrowing or pinpointing the opportunities. Nothing is more critical at this stage, and nothing takes more discipline.

In this section of the book, you'll come to learn that there are many different types of commercial real estate. We'll go through each one and you'll understand the pros and the cons, the cycles and the challenges. I'll do my best to provide you with all the facts that, when added to your own gut instincts, will land you on the right path to success.

Week 3

Exploring the Fundamentals

If you really do the hard work and you really make the tough decisions during the first two weeks (I know you will), it will be time to get down to brass tacks, as the saying goes, and start becoming an expert in your real estate type and the locations you have chosen. I'll show you how to make sense of the "action" that's been going on in your areas. We'll analyze what's sold, what "comps" are and what they mean, and I'll show you how to develop trend lines. Better yet, I'll show you how to interpret it all.

The key here is to understand where the market is right now so that you can understand where it is headed two or three years down the road. When you buy property, you buy it for the long term. This is a buy-and-hold book. I don't advocate flipping property, especially not commercial property. If you're in, then be in it for long-term appreciation and immediate cash flow.

By the end of the third week, you'll have developed a clear snapshot of what the market looks like, in your estimation. Those last three words—in your estimation—are an important qualifier. Later on, when you begin developing your network, you'll see how well your picture matches up with the veterans' opinion of the market. In order to talk with the veterans, you must have some market smarts—you want to be credible after all—and this week will begin that journey.

If you are really a motivated type, you can make more progress faster in these early weeks. Don't shortchange yourself here. Be sure you know all the answers to the questions asked during these weeks before moving on to weeks four and five. That's when the real work begins.

WEEKS 4 AND 5

ADVANCED RESEARCH

More research? You bet. Research never ends, because in the real world of real estate investing, the market is continually changing, new properties appear, cities and towns make improvements, neighborhoods decline, and economics change; I mean, things just keep shifting. For me, that's what keeps this life exciting and interesting. I like the challenge and I like winning. One of the reasons that I win more than most at real estate isn't because I'm smarter. It's because I do more research than most. Real estate is not an efficient market, so this is an area of potential advantage. There's no golden touch. Just do the work.

What exactly is advanced research and how does it differ from the stuff you did in week 3? Well, the next two weeks are all about comparing data. It's the time when you pin your view of the market against the experts' views of the market and compare it to the analytical data. Don't worry, you'll be ready. The goal, frankly, isn't necessarily to have all the right answers. The goal is to learn and develop your own expertise and grow your team of experts.

As in so many professions, those who are in a position to sell you something are in a position to teach you something as well. I've probably learned more from sales people than I've learned from teachers!

This is the first step in building your professional network, and that's pretty exciting. In this chapter of the book, I'll show you who are your best resources and what to ask. I'll make sure you walk in with loads of credibility. It's up to you to take it all in.

WEEK 6

FIND THE MONEY

It may seem too soon, but it isn't. It's time to line up investors and financing. You may be thinking you won't know enough, but believe me, as long as you don't take short-cuts in the process, you will. You may be thinking at this point, that there are a few properties you like but you don't have one that you're seriously considering. That's okay. You have to have your financing and investors lined up before you can become a serious buyer. So why wait? Start getting investors and financing now.

In this chapter, I'll show you how to meet with lenders and talk the basics. You'll learn how to get financing lined up, and what the terms will be. I'll also share the ins and outs of having private investors and how to find them. I've made the decision to include outside investors on all of my real estate holdings. There are pros and cons to this, but to me the pros outweigh the cons. You'll understand my reasons soon.

WEEK 7

NARROW YOUR OPTIONS AND PICK THE WINNERS

By Week 7, you'll have a handful of properties that look interesting. Interesting and worthy of your investment are two different things. So in this chapter, I'll show you how to fully analyze a property, to do what's called preliminary due diligence and establish a value.

Remember when I said you'll need that HP financial calculator? Well this is one of those times. You'll learn how to crunch the numbers that matter—the ones that signal opportunity or money pit. I mean that. My very first property that I ever looked at and came very close to buying crashed and burned late in the deal. You remember, that was my first $15,000 loss. If I had done my homework better in the beginning, I would have saved myself fifteen Gs.

Picking winners is a talent, and you'll want to work hard at perfecting it. It is the key to loving this business, making money, building wealth, and winning. You'll find there's no mystery to it. It's all about knowing as much as you can about the properties and making solid decisions based on those findings. You'll see.

WEEKS 8 AND 9

MAKE THE OFFER AND NEGOTIATE THE DEAL

By Week 7, you'll have analyzed the handful of properties that were on your short list. Now it's time to focus on the one, two, or three at the top. Start with number three as your first offer. It's a learning experience. Your final goal is to get the property you want at the price you want. So the way you learn is by making offers on properties you don't necessarily want, at prices you know the sellers won't accept. And don't worry, in this chapter, I'll explain exactly how to make that offer and negotiate the deal, complete with all its subtleties.

Making your first offer and going through your first negotiation is, without a doubt, the scariest and most exhilarating time in the whole process. It's the leap of faith, but actually, with this nine-week process, it's more a leap of knowledge.

DETAILED DUE DILIGENCE AND CLOSING

By this point, you are done with the nine-week process. But no book on real estate—at least no good book on real estate would end there. You simply must learn what you need to know about due diligence and closing.

You'll find after nine weeks, if you follow the process and make decisions based on the numbers, that this isn't really a leap at all. It's a solid decision based on rational evaluation. That's what any real estate investment should be; in truth, any investment, period. Too often emotion gets in the way. The "gorgeous" brownstone office building that's so "amazing." The powerful and prominent warehouse building that's a real "winner." Not always! Right now there is a million square feet of very unexciting tin shed industrial property that some friends of mine own free and clear. It throws off $2 million a year in cash flow. It isn't pretty or glamorous, but I know why the owners own it. You do, too. It makes them a lot of money!

Throughout this process you'll see how to avoid the emotional traps so that by the time you get to the offer, you'll be confidently excited. After all, your venture into real estate investing has to be fun and thrilling, but rational at the same time. When you enjoy the process and are confident, the money will come.

LEASE IT AND KEEP IT LEASED

Owning an investment property is good, but owning one that is fully leased is even better. This last section will show you what it takes to lease your property. We'll go into detail, but recognize I cover this subject in far more depth in my book *The Art of Commercial Real Estate Leasing*. People make careers out of leasing commercial buildings and in that book I share my knowledge and experiences. It's an important next read for you as you get into this business because leasing is not always an easy thing to do. That's why in this chapter, I advise you to work with a pro, but at the same time help you be a wise buyer of this service.

CHAPTER 4

FOCUS YOUR GOALS

WEEK 1 OF 9

At this point it's only fair to tell you that I set goals for just about everything. I'm a pathological goal setter, and I don't just set goals, I track and monitor their progress, adjusting my actions as needed to achieve them. Okay, call it a sickness, but there are worse obsessions, although my wife probably would have trouble coming up with what those are exactly.

Having goals has served me well in life. I'm living proof that you can achieve anything you want to achieve if you really want it badly enough and set goals to achieve it. I am working to achieve my goals financially, in business, personally, and with my family. When I hit any one goal, I establish another in that area of my life and keep on going.

This pattern has made my life exciting. When I set out to learn Tae Kwon Do—it was after baseball and after I achieved all I wanted in running—my goal was to earn a black belt. It was straightforward and, granted, highly optimistic, since I had never done any martial arts before. Twelve years later, I was a third degree black belt and a world champion. That's the power of goals, perseverance, and having a path. Clearly, none of it would have been possible without first having the goal.

Today, while I have gold medals on the wall in my office, the most important badges are the experiences and the confidence that can come only through accomplishment. Starting your own commercial real estate investment business may very well be your Tae Kwon Do. It may be that thing that, once you get into it and start accomplishing, will only fuel your confidence and your ability to do more.

There are two kinds of people in this world: those who dream and those who act. The difference between them is vast. This chapter will help you narrow your dreams so that taking action won't be so daunting. What holds back many dreamers is that acting on those dreams seems overwhelming, complicated, and confusing. So in this chapter, not only will we work to establish your real estate goals, but you'll begin to see how the rest of the nine weeks is really an action plan to achieving them.

A CLEAR PICTURE OF REALITY

Jack Welch, the former CEO of General Electric and best-selling business author, has an axiom: "Face reality as it is, not as it was or as you wish it to be." He's absolutely right. Facing reality as it is allows you to look at the root cause of where you are. To me, this is one of the most important concepts in the book because once you gain clarity within your goals, you will have clarity on how to proceed.

Dan Sullivan, founder of The Strategic Coach® and my personal coach for more than a decade, says change begins by telling the truth, and you will have to do that for yourself and those around you. Setting goals can't happen in isolation. Think of the entire exercise as a team event. Meet with your spouse, your partner, or best friend. Get a sense of reality in terms of your finances. If you're broke, investing is going to be hard. Take a good, honest look at the root issues that have gotten you to this place. Is it a career that is going nowhere? Is it an inability to do the things you want to do in life? Is it spending habits that are out of control? The more honest you are about the root issues—the real causes—for where you are in your life, the better you can attack and correct those issues.

My daughter can help me clarify the point. One day, her cherished iPod was stolen. So, being a good dad, I got her another one. Within a few weeks, that one was stolen, too. Now without an iPod and no chance of her father buying her another one (I'm not crazy), she borrowed her brother's iPod. When he wanted it back, she got angry. Her anger was toward her brother for taking back his iPod, but the real problem is that she keeps getting her iPod stolen. Once she corrects the root issue—taking better care of her things—she'll be ready to have another iPod.

This kind of brutal honesty isn't easy for kids to hear. It isn't easy for adults to accept, either. As you reflect on your goal setting, be honest with yourself and identify the root issue for where you are in your life, and do the work of correcting it. It will make your goals all the more valid, worthwhile, and attainable.

WHAT DOES A REAL ESTATE GOAL LOOK LIKE?

A goal must be written, specific, attainable, and have a deadline. I have friends who are always trying to hit the home runs out of the park. They say they want to own a plane, so they go after every long shot deal in a desperate attempt to round up the cash to achieve their lofty goal. I don't see them as smart investors; I see them as people who play the lottery, hoping to win and win big.

Commercial real estate investing is a great business if you have a long-term horizon. There are no short cuts to success. I wish there were. In truth, longevity in a business helps you gain wisdom, and once you do that, you have attained the unfair advantage and things get fun. You start to be able to see the future.

Let me tell you how I found and bought the house I'm living in right now. Even though this is a residential real estate story in a commercial real estate investing book, it serves as a good example of knowing what you want and going after it. Furthermore, this is exactly the same process I use to set goals in my commercial real estate investing business, in my personal life, and in my family life.

By the time my wife and I had our fourth child, we knew we would need a bigger home. I had done the soul searching required to know what I wanted in life and included my wife in the process. We wanted a place to raise our children, and a place where we could spend time with them. Because I felt driving to and from work was a huge waste of time, I knew I wanted a home within a two-mile radius of my office. So the first thing I did was draw North, South, East, and West boundaries on a map. That set the general location. Next came the house itself. It had to have at least four bedrooms because of our kids. I wanted to have a backyard mountain view because the real estate investor in me knows that homes with views appreciate faster than homes without. Finally, I wanted at least an acre property with a big back yard because in Phoenix they are rare and, again, it would help our home appreciate in value faster over the long term. I had a target price range in which I felt a home like the one I was searching for would realistically cost. There were other things we wanted the house to have, like a certain number of baths and outdoor amenities, but these were the must haves.

In short, I wanted a house that we could enjoy living in, but that I knew was set up to appreciate over time. I knew that this would be a big investment, and I wanted to do it right. I wasn't willing to sacrifice the appreciation and long-term value to get the features I wanted for comfort. That would have been an emotional decision, and to me real estate cannot and should not be an emotional purchase.

After researching every house in my geographic radius that met my specific criteria, I found only thirteen matches, and none of them were for sale. Sounds like an impossible situation, right? Not at all. It just meant I had to launch into action. That meant contacting each homeowner.

My first contact took the form of a personal note to each of the home owners telling them that I wanted to raise my kids in this neighborhood and that we would be living here a long time. I told each homeowner

I wanted to buy his or her home and then personally hand delivered each note with one of my kids in tow. These people were friendly. We talked history, that we were from the area, and that my wife grew up in this neighborhood and went to the schools nearby. All of which was true. After talking with each homeowner and given a space of time, three of them eventually were interested. After a few months one was willing to sell. The bidding was between us and another family and to be honest, we got the house because the homeowner felt the most comfortable with us. She knew we'd take great care of her home, raise our kids and keep the neighborhood up.

Dear Arcadia Home Owner:

My name is Craig Coppola. My wife, Tracy and I are looking to purchase a home, a specific home, in Arcadia. The home we are looking for needs to be located on the north side of a quiet street, with a large lot. Your house fits our requirements. If you have been thinking of selling, I would appreciate it greatly if you would consider calling me first.

We have four children (two at Hopi and two younger ones) and have literally outgrown our three bedroom, 2300 square foot house.

We are motivated to buy, flexible, and can buy without any qualification period. We own our current home debt free. We can move immediately or buy and lease back. If selling is of interest to you, or if you know of a neighbor who is interested in selling their home, please call.

Thank you for your time.

Sincerely,

R. Craig Coppola

Today, we still live in this house, and it has more than doubled in value. Compare that with how most people buy houses. They have a vague idea of what they want, they waste huge amounts of time driving around, picking up flyers, looking at homes that seldom measure up, calling realtors, and finally choosing one that is the "closest" they can find to what they actually think they wanted.

The letter, while certainly significant later in the nine-week program, is the least important part of the story here. The most important part is how I knew exactly what I wanted with such certainty that I was able to go to such lengths with such commitment to move a homeowner who was not considering selling to actually sell her home. That's the lesson that I've carried throughout all my real estate investing and in everything I do in life. Pinpoint goal-setting is a learned behavior. You can do it, too.

YOUR PERSONAL FINANCIAL FREEDOM PLAN: FOCUS, NARROW, DEFINE

For me, personal goal setting and planning has always been about focusing, narrowing, and defining what I want, then pinpointing that one thing with such complete accuracy and such a vivid picture that there is no doubt. Doing that takes asking yourself basic questions about who you are, what you can tolerate, how committed you are, how long you're willing to wait, and what you're willing to sacrifice.

Self-awareness is the key, and I gain clarity by beginning with the end in mind. What do you want your life to be like now? Five years from now? Ten years from now? This is all relevant. The most relevant picture when it comes to real estate goal-setting is a ten-year goal. Seeing the future out that far will help define your "now" and your "five years from now" picture. Once you have an idea of what your "ten years from now" image looks like, you can see if the sacrifices you'll have to make from today forward are acceptable to you.

When I go through this exercise—and I go through this continually— my goal is always to achieve financial freedom. Financial freedom meant something different when I was single, something different once I got married, and something different with every child we had. It's constantly changing, and I am constantly adjusting. That's the way life is. Expect your goals to change, but just because they do doesn't mean they aren't worth having right now.

Financial freedom to me breaks down into expenses, net worth, and passive income. Passive income is money that I do not have to work for and comes to me via my investments. Of course, the net worth and passive income amounts that made up my original goal and the ones that make up my goal today were and are very specific. I also have a definite timetable I am working against. Actually, a big part of my motivation for setting the financial freedom goal wasn't about money. It was about time. I wanted to have more of it for my kids as they entered school. I wanted to coach Little League and go to my kids' sporting events and plays. I also wanted to have the time to pursue my own personal interests like running and martial arts and, today, backpacking. Sure, I knew it would take years to get to the point where I would be that free. It did. The trade off was that I would not be around much when the kids were babies. Was it hard? Yes, but not as hard as it would be now to miss my eleven-year-old daughter's soccer game, or to not coach Little League All Stars.

I chose to do whatever I had to do when my kids were young to make sure I was there as they got more active. My wife was on board with that. It comes back to the pain of discipline versus the pain of regret. It's hard to discipline yourself to work long hours, nights, and weekends for years at a time, missing out on times with family and friends. The pain of that kind of discipline is real when it's happening. When it's over, the pain is fleeting. Certainly it's a memory of hard work, but it's hardly painful. In fact, the accomplishment feels good and has contributed to whom I have become. The pain of regret, on the other hand, isn't immediate. It comes tomorrow, next week, next year, or fifteen years down the road, and once it's here there's no going back. It's hard to soothe. That's the pain of regret, and it can last the rest of your life.

My financial freedom goal continues to change, and I continue to do the things I must to achieve it. The cool part is that even though I am still actively working, I've set my life up to be there for my kids, to travel the world, to pursue interests like Tae Kwon Do and backpacking. Aiming high has a way of doing that. It takes you further, faster. My time is important to me, and I have the freedom to schedule around *my* calendar instead of *others'* calendars. My plan is working. I don't share this personal story to brag or to let on that I am any better than anyone else. I'm telling it because success isn't just for the lucky or the privileged. It's for everyone—regular people like me included—once you know what you want.

Setting your personal goal will take some soul-searching. Here is a tool and some examples that will help you as you seek to discover what you want out of life from a financial perspective. Only by doing that can you develop a real estate investment goal, an important step to helping you achieve it.

MY FINANCIAL FREEDOM PLAN

Your financial freedom plan provides direction, purpose, and context for your real estate investments. It provides the "why" behind the "what" and helps you focus your goals.

My Vision: _____
This is a clear mental picture of your financially independent future.

Goals: _____
These are measurable objectives for becoming a real estate investor.

My Strategies: _____
This is a specific approach to achieving the goals.

Assemble into Your Financial Freedom Plan Statement: _____
_____

So far in this chapter, I have alluded to my mission, vision, values, goals, strategies, and tactics. We've discussed many of the results. Here are a few examples of Financial Freedom Plan statements to get you thinking:

By 2019, I want to be financially free by having $50,000 a month in passive income.

My vision is to become a real estate investor so I can travel more, have more time to spend with my family, and within five years generate at least $100,000 per year in passive income, with assets that are growing to fund my retirement.

I want to diversify my investments and gain an average return of 15 percent annually so that I can achieve my retirement goal of $3 million by year-end 2020.

You may find these helpful as you develop your own goals. Note how specific and vivid they are. The more specific you can be, the better you'll be able to take action and know when you have arrived.

Don't worry if you can't complete this form in one sitting. I recommend getting as much information as you can commit to paper on the first go around, and then let it rest. Look at it daily and modify as you work your way through your week. You'll find countless triggers during your day that will help bring clarity to what you really want out of life. And remember, just because you write all this down doesn't mean it won't change as time passes. It absolutely will. Think of this as a snapshot, a benchmark, from which to begin.

YOUR REAL ESTATE GOAL:
THE FOUR PARAMETERS

Clearly, having a bigger vision, a vision of financial freedom, is important. It keeps you motivated during those challenging times and gives the work you do relevance. You'll need more than just a vision of financial freedom to make it a reality. Achievement means getting very specific. It means focusing on a smaller step: your first investment in a commercial property.

Just as you will be working on a broader financial freedom plan, you'll want to begin working on your commercial real estate investment goals. Here's the simplest way of establishing those goals—simply narrow your choices using the following four parameters:

Product Type: Choose between office, retail, multi-family, and a host of others in the commercial real estate sector. In the next chapter, we describe the pros and cons of each.

Location: We talked a lot about this already. This is the most important parameter because location is the biggest indicator of a property's future performance.

Money: How much money will you have to invest or put into a real estate deal? Be realistic—and remember, it shouldn't be your first investment dollar.

Investment Structure: Do you want to go solo or bring in some investor partners? The choice is yours.

The form that follows will help you organize your thoughts.

MY FIRST COMMERCIAL REAL ESTATE
INVESTMENT GOAL

Use the four parameters below to pinpoint exactly the kind of investment opportunity you are interested in. The more specific you can be, the better.

The <u>product type</u> I want to own is:_____

Narrow to the kind of property you think you want to own.

My preferred <u>location</u> is: _____

Decide in what part of town you want your property.

The <u>money</u> I have to invest is: _____

Decide how much money you want to invest in this venture.

My preferred <u>investment structure</u> is: _____

Determine whether or not you want investors or partners.

Assemble into your goal statement:_____

Here are a few examples of Commercial Real Estate Investment Goals:

I have $12,000 to buy my first office building in Phoenix, Arizona by December 31, 20XX.

I have $5,000 to invest in another investor's real estate deal to learn the process. After I do this, I will become a managing partner in a commercial real estate deal by March 31, 20XX.

I will pay off all my credit card debt by June 1, 20XX, and while doing so become an expert in one specific market niche—mini-storage in the airport submarket—in preparation for my first real estate investment in 20XX.

To this day, I still think about the four parameters to narrow down my next investment project, and for me, the location parameter is the most important. This is a simple yet helpful tool. You'll find real estate is less about *finding something* that can make you money, and more about *narrowing down* the options until you arrive at the best one that can make you money. There's a big difference. Finding the right investment has an element of chance and implies that there is only one right investment. Narrowing down the options until you locate the best one puts you in control, implies that there are lots of good opportunities out there, and prepares you when a great opportunity comes your way. I know there are lots of opportunities.

FOCUS YOUR GOALS RIGHT NOW

There's no time like the present, so use the forms in this chapter or create your own using the ones in this book as a guide. Remember all that talk about action? It's time to take some right now.

Put your plan and your goal into one notebook or keep them in a separate folder on your computer. The key is keeping everything together and dated so you can live what you've written. Make your life plan and your commercial real estate investing goal something you commit to on paper, so they are solid and real. Be as descriptive as you can be so there's passion and life there. Reviewing a vivid goal will help you get through the challenges. We do actually achieve what we think about, but we also must *act* on what we think about. Writing down your plan and your goal is a critical first action.

PREPARING FOR WEEK 2

While you are developing your Financial Freedom Plan and your first real estate goal, you'll also want to prepare for Week 2, when you'll get the lay of the land in your local market. You'll need a full tank of gas, a block of time during the week, and a block of time on the weekend, so try to keep your schedule light. That weekend tee time, barbeque, or shopping trip may have to wait.

CHAPTER 5

LEARN YOUR LOCAL REAL ESTATE LANDSCAPE

WEEK 2 OF 9

Welcome to Week 2. By this point you have your first financial freedom plan and your commercial real estate investment goal on paper and in mind as you begin the journey of becoming a real estate investor. Don't be surprised if your plan changes as you go through the nine weeks. Plans do that—they're supposed to—they should be alive, growing, changing. Last week was a start. You have a deadline of nine weeks to make it happen. You also have a good idea of the real estate investment you'd like to make in terms of the four parameters introduced in the last chapter. Your picture might look something like this:

> *Financial Freedom Plan: By 20XX, I will have attained financial freedom by having $5 million in commercial real estate which I own, manage, and control that will provide $50,000 a year in passive income, allowing me to fund my kids' college educations and spend more time doing the things I enjoy.*

Real Estate Goal: By December 31, 20XX, I will own public mini-storage properties where I invest $50,000 of my own money and raise $250,000 in equity for one or two properties in the west side of town.

Your mission in Week 2 is to get the lay of the land in your market and be in a position to refine and affirm the real estate portion of your goal to perhaps two or three product types in two or three viable locations. Perhaps your goal-setting was so successful that you know exactly the kind of commercial property you are most interested in and even the specific part of town. Excellent! During Week 2, we'll open up the options a bit and help you either affirm your decision or adjust it slightly based on the market. After all, your real estate goals are simply the vehicle for you to achieve your bigger life plan. We want to make sure you are set up for success. Understanding the market in which you live, work, and plan to operate is a big part of that.

When I began investing, it wasn't hard at all for me to select commercial office as my property type of choice. It was nearly impossible, however, to know what the size of the transaction would be, the time commitment, the amount of capital, and how to put it all together. In fact, I was not the managing member of the first several deals I invested in. I invested money in other people's projects just to learn the game. There was a lot to know, and it was a good first step. Later, I discovered that everyone is human, and there are no magic wands that can cast a spell of success. It didn't take long before I had formed *my own* opinions about how to select and manage properties. That's when I knew it was time to take the lead and go out on my own. I decided that my property investments would be ones that I found and managed.

THE LAY OF THE LAND—THE NEIGHBORHOOD

Even if you have lived in your city or town all your life and you know every road and every building, humor me and still hop in your car and take a ride. This won't be a ride to simply look at buildings; it's a ride to help you look at your town or city with "real estate eyes."

Actually looking at the buildings is a minor thing at this point. This drive will help you to understand the environment the buildings are in from many different perspectives. The drive is about location, location, location.

Start your drive with the goal of trying to understand the overall city from a land/real estate investment perspective. Be observant. What do you think is impacting real estate values in one neighborhood or another? Even if you think you know the area in which you want to invest, it's still a good idea to understand what's going on in other areas of your city or town. That will play a part in the value of the area you like best as much as anything else.

We are all creatures of habit. We drive the same way to work and the same way home, day in and day out. Not only do we miss the opportunities on that drive, we never see the changes that are taking place in the other 90 percent of our community. So the first thing I recommend: drive a different way to go to work. If you normally take the highway, take the surface streets. If you always stop at the same Starbucks for coffee, go to a different one. Take in a variety of scenery and people.

Once you think you know an area, travel there at different times of the day. How about evenings, weekends, and at night? Really take the time to see how people live in this area, how it is trafficked. You may be surprised. There are neighborhoods that not only have changed over the years, but even through the course of a day. I've seen parts of town that are happening spots during the week and during lunch, but are absolute ghost towns during the dinner hour and at night. If you're looking for a great building for a daytime business, this could be your spot. If you're looking for a building for an evening business, look elsewhere. Your goal here is to look at an area and "get it." This means you get what it's about and you know what kinds of businesses are good fits. Once you see an area and get it, you will begin to be able to see the future. This is a gut response that you should write down. You'll have an opportunity later to test how right you are when you talk to the experts.

When it comes to understanding the environment, I look for what real estate pros call "the path of growth" in the market. Even in cities that, as a whole, are not growing, there are usually areas that are. How do you recognize the path of growth when it comes to commercial real estate? Look for where home builders are buying land, where new homes are being constructed, and where elementary schools are planned and being built. The city government is a great resource for this information. Their staffs and records can tell you where they are planning to build new facilities and where infrastructure is going in. You can also get good insight from the economic development officials in your city offices. It's always interesting to see which projects they are the most excited about and what they see coming on line down the road.

City officials often can be very excited about urban revitalization projects that are underway. Sometimes they even help fund projects that jump start the process. How exciting it is to think about being part of the solution to violence and crime and urban blight! Here's my caution: these kinds of projects take time, lots of time. Not only is there the obvious planning, zoning, designing, and entitlement process that must happen, but sometimes votes are involved. Then there is the intangible consumer acceptance variable that can take years. In my hometown of Phoenix, there was more than $400 million of revitalization projects built before I considered one of them an area for investment. The elapsed time was more than twelve years. There's no need to be first. Stay cautious for a very long time because even neighborhoods marked for revitalization may remain in decline for years.

I should point out that some real estate investors make it their entire business to seek out declining neighborhoods. People who specialize in urban revitalization are just one example. That's not my area of interest or expertise, so for my specialty, commercial office space, I stay clear when I see a lot of graffiti or closed businesses. That seems obvious, but you'll be surprised how a quaint historic home, recently rezoned commercial, in a troubled neighborhood, can still be compelling to emotional investors. They can easily talk themselves into a bad decision by thinking that buying this building will be good for the neighborhood, or by telling themselves they can live with the location because the building is so perfect. Neither of these arguments is good enough. Remember, it's location first, no matter how difficult the dwelling is to pass up.

The reason I'm such a stickler on this point is that it's really hard to grow your way out of a downhill slide. There's a difference between a declining area and an area that is going to be revitalized. When you get the feel that a neighborhood is going downhill, stay away. If it's on the upswing and that historic building is right in the center of it, don't let your preconceived beliefs about the neighborhood hold you back. There may be an opportunity. Understand they call it *real estate* for a reason. You're looking at the real estate first. That's the key underlying truth to all of this. The building is second.

To me, an absolute must is to fully understand where the market is going, not just where it is today. It's all about feel and not getting in too early. What I mean by that is, unlike some businesses where speed is everything, there is no need to be on the bleeding edge in real estate. You don't have to be first. You don't want to be first; leave that to the biggest players, who can afford the risk. There's plenty of opportunity and money to be made by being second, third, and even twenty-third. Leave the bleeding edge to the big boys. In fact, if you're a small investor who is starting out, never be first.

Even though time flies, when it comes to real estate, I've been surprised by how long it takes the future to actually occur. You may find out your view of the future is ten years ahead of the curve. My rule is to take my time and be patient. There's no need for excessive urgency at this point in the process. If there's room for one person to make money in an area, there's room for more. In fact, I've found there are very few properties that are so special that if you miss them, you miss the deal of the century. While those properties do exist, their owners know it and they typically overprice the properties anyway, negating the value of the deal. A good example is The Esplanade and the Biltmore Fashion Square; both within the same city block in the highly sought after Camelback Corridor. Those properties are the types that are bought by huge institutions who want trophy properties where the look and the location are more critical than the solidity of the real estate and the return. Another example occurred when GE bought Hayden Ferry Lakeside in a prestigious area of Tempe, Arizona. MetLife bought the Esplanade in Phoenix. These are called Core Plus Properties and are named such because they create a portfolio of foundation projects that entice other investors looking for glamorous investments.

As you look at neighborhoods, don't overlook the places that you think might be too expensive, too cheap, or that used to be blighted. Neighborhoods change. I know one investor who has made a ton of money improving the looks and performance of less-than-stellar buildings and increasing the property values. It takes a big commitment to do that, but she's doing it. Understand, there are also slumlords out there who have made big bucks owning very shabby properties. That's not something I encourage; part of what we can do as investors is create better spaces for all. But with that said, it's a free country.

Everyone always asks, "What are the warning signs of a declining neighborhood?" That's easy, and if you go with your feelings, you'll know it instinctively. True story: I was driving in the morning one day checking out a few neighborhoods I hadn't been through in a while and drove right by a car on blocks with the tires missing. That's a bad sign. So are multiple cars parked in the street at night and a tenant mix in a building that looks fly-by-night or that are in shady businesses. Finally, take a look at the general upkeep. If the properties are unkempt, that's not good, either. You may even want to take a look at the police reports to see how much crime happens in the area.

The bottom line is, you can modify your building but you, alone, can't modify the neighborhood. And about that quaint historic building in a seedy part of town: sure it would make great offices for a trendy design studio, but if your employees are too afraid to work there or stay after hours, how wise was your decision? Open your eyes, think through what you're seeing, and listen to your gut. Write down what you feel—yes, what you *feel*—about every neighborhood. Following is a form that will not only help you know important considerations, but also give you a place to record your impressions about the area.

The Nine-Weeks Drive Guide — The Neighborhood Environment

Below are the things you need to look for as you drive neighborhoods and look at environments (Rating scale: 1 is poor, 2 is fair, 3 is average, 4 is good, 5 is very good). Add comments to right.

Neighborhood Environment: _____ *(list area)*

Border: N_____ / S_____ / E_____ / W_____

(Comments)

Overall upkeep	1	2	3	4	5 _____
General condition of buildings	1	2	3	4	5 _____
Quality/condition of cars in area	1	2	3	4	5 _____
Quality of businesses in area	1	2	3	4	5 _____
Traffic patterns	1	2	3	4	5 _____
Area landscape	1	2	3	4	5 _____
Overall visual interest	1	2	3	4	5 _____
Perceived prestige	1	2	3	4	5 _____

Would I buy here? Yes No If yes, what product type? _____

On what street(s) would I own? _____

Your Feelings and Impressions:

High points?	Morning	Noon	Night
	_____	_____	_____
	_____	_____	_____

Low points?	Morning	Noon	Night
	_____	_____	_____
	_____	_____	_____

Future outlook?

In 5 years _____
_____
_____
_____

In 10 years _____
_____
_____
_____

Other Impressions: _____
_____
_____
_____

Questions I need answered: _____
_____
_____
_____

THE BUILDINGS AT LAST!

As I mentioned, the buildings themselves are practically the last things I look at when I'm getting familiar with a city and its neighborhoods. Even when it comes to actual buildings, I don't initially see the vertical structure; I see the property it's sitting on. Are there enough parking spaces? Is it easy to get into and out of? In other words, does the property have good access? Looking at the building and the site it is sitting on, does it feel right and can visitors find the location without getting lost?

From there, I take a closer look at who is occupying the building. What are the tenants like—are they quality, established companies or a little on the flaky side? A tenant doesn't have to be Home Depot or Taco Bell to be acceptable. A local nonprofit outfit that's been in a building for ten years is actually a good tenant; especially when compared to, let's say, a start-up technology company that no one has ever heard of, with millions in venture capital money and a burn rate of a million dollars per month, with one customer and no profits. I also consider the tenant's position within their industry, the level of competition, and where the industry is going.

One afternoon several years ago, I had a friend call me from her car as she was traveling in a small town some distance from her home. She said, "Hey Craig, I'm looking at a great building here all set up for a call center. What do you think?" For me, the answer was easy. Call centers are declining in the U.S., with most companies shipping their operations overseas. I replied, "Unless you're in India right now, I'd pass." Much of this is really common sense and knowing where the trends are, not just in real estate, but in the areas of business and life that affect real estate.

The following tracking form is a tool you can use to record your first-glance view and impressions of a property. It's also a great idea to bring along a digital camera or smartphone so you can take photos of buildings and attach them to the Drive Guide records. Pay special notice to the items below and be sure to record your overall impressions as well.

The Nine-Weeks Drive Guide — The Building

Below are the things you need to look for as you drive and look at buildings. You'll want one form for each building you view (Rating scale: 1 is poor, 2 is fair, 3 is average, 4 is good, 5 is very good).

Building Name: _____

Building Address: _____

(Comments)

Location within area	1	2	3	4	5	_____
Curb appeal	1	2	3	4	5	_____
General condition	1	2	3	4	5	_____
Parking	1	2	3	4	5	_____
Lighting	1	2	3	4	5	_____
Access/entrance and exit	1	2	3	4	5	_____
Tenants	1	2	3	4	5	_____
Ease of finding	1	2	3	4	5	_____
Landscaping	1	2	3	4	5	_____
Fits with your needs/wants	1	2	3	4	5	_____

Your Feelings and Impressions:

High points?	Morning	Noon	Night
	_____	_____	_____
	_____	_____	_____

Low points?	Morning	Noon	Night
	_____	_____	_____
	_____	_____	_____

Future outlook?

In 5 years _____
_____
_____
_____

In 10 years _____
_____
_____
_____

Of course, there are plenty of exceptions to every rule, but with your first investment, it's a good idea to stick with the rules before you break them. Later, when you've not only developed your knowledge but also your instincts and your wealth, you can afford to take a few more calculated risks.

THE COMMERCIAL ASSET CLASS OPTIONS

When you decided the type of commercial real estate that most appealed to you in the last chapter, did you consider all the options? Most likely not, because so few people really know all the commercial real estate options available. It's important to see the commercial real estate market in its entirety so that you get an accurate picture of how it is all interconnected.

Here they are, complete with descriptions and the risks and the rewards:

Multi-Family: Multi-family includes everything from small, duplex apartment buildings to entire apartment complexes with 800 units or more. The biggest risk in this asset class is over-supply, because when people have lots of choices, rents can fall, affecting operating performance and cash flow. Another risk with multi-family is that when interest rates are low, more people can afford to buy homes, so they don't have to rent. That leaves more apartment units vacant and competing for fewer residents. On the plus side, when lending gets tighter and it becomes harder to qualify for a home mortgage, renting becomes the only option and the demand for apartment homes increases. Investors have made a lot of money in this area of commercial real estate by buying right and managing efficiently. Like all commercial real estate, the value of a multi-family property increases based on increased operating performance. In other words, buying a property and then managing and leasing it better than the previous owner can create an automatic bump in value. That puts the owner in control of his or her asset, which is why I love real estate.

Retail: Retail commercial space is something you know probably quite well: shopping centers, strip centers, malls, and stand-alone retailers. The benefit with retail property is that construction costs are high, making for a high barrier to entry by competitors. This keeps demand usually ahead of supply. Speaking as an investor, that's generally a good position to be in. It's not all blue sky. Economic factors such as reports of inflation, recession, and declining consumer spending trends can trigger retailers to go out of business, and, as a building owner, you could lose a retail tenant. You must base your success on a value that is somewhere below 100 percent occupancy, because retailers can come and go. Competition can also turn a favored retail center into one that is second-class. That's what I mean about seeing the future. You want to know what is coming up, not just what is.

Commercial Office: Office buildings and office condos make up one of the largest real estate asset classes. Just look around. We all work somewhere, and it's offices that house many of us from eight to five. In this sector, leases tend to be long term, which can provide some stability. Offices come in many shapes and sizes, so there is diversity and easy entry for new investors. Some offices are former residential buildings converted to office space. Others are conventional office buildings of all shapes and sizes. The benefit of commercial office space is that there is likely something in your town that will fit your budget as a first-time investor and give you plenty of room to grow as you increase your wealth and your level of investment.

Industrial: Just like commercial office buildings, industrial buildings tend to have longer leases and lots of options when it comes to investing. There are giant warehouses with upwards of 500,000 square feet and smaller mixed-use spaces in the neighborhood of 3,000 square feet, along with everything in-between. Industrial space is a classic first-time investor property because of the many options available. Many first-time investors also have their own businesses and need this kind of space.

Health Care: This asset class in commercial real estate includes not just hospitals, but also nursing homes, medical buildings, and assisted living facilities. The benefit of this class is that recessions and economic downturns don't really affect it much, but it is prone to the ups and downs of the tenant. Medical practices are small businesses. Hospitals are big businesses. Business can fluctuate. Plus, the medical profession is one that is in a state of flux, and will be so for years to come. Through my experience in this area, I know that not only is it important to have the right tenants in your space, it's important to have the right mix of tenants in your space—the right practices and the right practitioners. Assisted-living facilities, on the other hand, are all about management. Having a reputable management company that specializes in these kinds of communities is a must.

Self-Storage: Self-storage are those mini-warehouse consumer and commercial storage facilities that you most likely have seen in your town. You may even have some of your things stored in one of them. They are seemingly recession resistant, and that is a big advantage for you as an investor. Generally, management is relatively easy. Believe it or not, corporations are actually the biggest users of storage facilities, and every year they pay billions to store excess files, records, and general stuff. The down side is that building self-storage facilities is a low-cost proposition. That means it's easy for competitors to break into the market, charge a lower price, and erode your margins. When it comes to self-storage, I always make sure there are lots of rooftops nearby as well. Ordinary people like you and I use self-storage, too.

Hospitality: This asset class includes hotels, motels, casinos, bed and breakfasts, resorts, and vacation rentals. Like assisted-care facilities, management is everything. In general, this is the asset class most closely connected with the health of the economy. In periods of economic decline, travel for business or pleasure is one of the early casualties of cost cutting and penny pinching. That affects the number of nights booked, which means per-night room rates can fall as properties vie for fewer customers. This erodes income and profitability, but in markets with a balanced supply and demand ratio, hospitality can be very lucrative.

Within each of these asset classes are sub-categories. All these options may at first seem overwhelming, but in reality it's this diversity that makes commercial real estate so lucrative and why smart investors specialize. This specialization enables us to have an advantage over other types of investments and over other types of investors who are trying to do it all.

THE REAL ESTATE CYCLE REVEALED

You'll notice that not only are there more kinds of commercial property than you could have imagined, their performance over time is cyclical in whole and in part. What I mean by that is; as I mentioned in the last section, each asset class runs through a cycle. Each asset class's cycle either flows before, flows with, or flows after another asset class's cycle.

For example, you'll find that growth in residential housing will fuel a similar but slightly lagging rise in retail. It makes sense when you consider that new homeowners will want shopping centers, grocery stores, and other conveniences near where they live. The surge in retail then drives growth in industrial and distribution, so that means warehouse and mixed-use property development grows. Home development also drives some growth in commercial office space, but again commercial lags behind. That's why when housing development slows, it takes a few years for commercial to slow down, too. You've probably noticed that. When the news is talking about real estate declines, it seems new commercial projects are still getting underway. That's another reason why I like commercial office as a property type. It has that long lag, so you can see the future coming based on the other property types' performance.

Real estate is all about cycles and their inevitability. That's why we will pay attention to this concept and help you understand how to recognize where you are in the cycle, formulate an action plan to take best advantage of the cycles, and make the best decisions.

Cycles are important, but if you buy right your real estate will do well, regardless of where things are in the cycle. In the beginning, buying right won't be as intuitive to you, so this cycle becomes golden. The diagram below shows the typical commercial real estate cycle and how it affects new construction and vacancy.

Market Cycle Quadrants

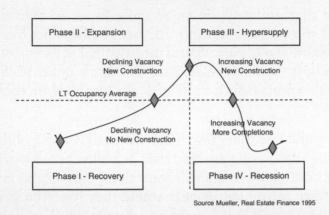

Source Mueller, Real Estate Finance 1995

This diagram shows a classic real estate cycle. In Phase 1, the lower left quadrant, the market is in recovery phase. There is declining vacancy and no new construction. You know the market is in this phase when there is some growth in the market indicated by properties being rented and properties being sold. Unlike when you are investing in the stock market or other efficient investment, this up trend will last a long time, years even. There is no need to rush into an investment. I don't like surprises, so I generally let the bigger guys make the first leaps during this phase. Then I make my moves with solid knowledge about the properties I am going after.

As you'll see in a minute when we talk about Phase 3 and Phase 4, declining markets aren't the time to take vacations. Doing lots of homework then will make you smarter and at the ready during a Phase 1 market. When the other guys who bought poorly in one of the other phases have thrown in the towel, that's when I buy.

During Phase 2, you see the occupancy rates move below the long-term occupancy ("LT Occupancy" line on the diagram), which is defined as the percentage of space occupied on average at a given time for your market. For example, a long-term occupancy of 80 percent says that the commercial real estate in a specific market is 80 percent occupied. Every market is different, but, in most cases, vacancy is very healthy when it is below 10 percent. Understand that new construction tends to start when vacancy rates drop below 10 and 15 percent, so during this phase new properties begin coming on line. Again, this phase of the cycle does not last days, weeks, or months. It tends to last a few years, so there is no hurry here either. If and when I buy during this phase, I make sure the numbers really work and that the property meets my qualifications. There's no way of knowing when the market is on the top or how long it will last, so caution is the rule here. If you're going to sell, Phase 2 is when you do it.

In Phase 3, the market is in obvious decline. The guessing game, however, is how far the market will fall and how long it will take. If you bought in Phase 1, you may have bought yourself some strength, but when you are still seeing new construction underway and occupancy rates increasing above the long-term occupancy for your market, the signs say that you are in Phase 3. This is known as hyper-supply. Obviously, I never buy during this phase no matter how badly I want a building. I am simply not willing to ride the wave to the bottom, not knowing how far down bottom is. What's the point when I know that there will be plenty of time for deals that make sense in Phase 1? In fact, I'll be buying the properties others foolishly bought in Phase 3. Except, I'll be buying them at bargain prices! You'll hear people say that there are buying opportunities in every phase. That is true, but it just depends on how strong your constitution is and how deep your pockets are.

Finally, Phase 4 signals market bottom. There's good news in Phase 4, too. The darker it gets in Phase 4, the better the buying opportunities will be in Phase 1. So if you're on the buying side, relish Phase 4 and take the time to look at properties. Look a lot, but don't buy a thing. There's no way of knowing the bottom until the market makes the turn upward. You'll know you're there when vacancy hits its high well above the long-term occupancy and buildings are no longer under construction. The cranes and bulldozers will be replaced by completed buildings sitting vacant. At this time, I do a lot of research so that when Phase I kicks in, I have pinpointed some ripe buying opportunities. I have lined up investors and financing and spoken to lots of people, telling them I'll give them a call when the turnaround happens.

While it is helpful to know that real estate is cyclical and in all cases interconnected by asset class, knowing where you are in a market cycle and predicting where it is going is key. Savvy investors can make money anywhere in the cycle, but it takes great skill and experience to make money on the right side of the quadrant. Furthermore, understand that all real estate follows this pattern, but that some asset classes will follow the curve earlier or later than another. For instance, residential real estate is always the first to decline and the first to rebound. Multi-family follows a little later, and retail and commercial after that. Commercial/industrial is usually the last asset class to emerge from a down market; however, it is usually the last to enter it. The more familiar you get with watching the real estate cycles, the better you will get at knowing where you are in it. Commercial real estate, for me, gives me plenty of warning to buy, sell, and hold.

A FEW ABCS

As I mentioned, understanding what comprises the various asset classes and some of the nuances of each will help you discover your options. Within each of the commercial property options we discussed earlier in this chapter are four classes that refer to the quality of the property. The class guidelines are as follows:

Class A+: Landmark quality, high-rise building with a central business district location. These are the best of the Class A buildings.

Class A: Buildings 100,000 square feet or bigger with at least five floors. Construction is concrete and steel, new construction. Buildings include business/support amenities like restaurants and banks and strong identifiable location and access.

Class B: Renovated buildings in good locations or newer buildings that are smaller in size. Can be wood-frame construction in non-prime location. Most first-time investors invest here.

Class C: Older buildings that are not renovated, of any size, in average to fair condition.

Perhaps you've seen these letters listed on brokerage signs: "class A," "class B," "class C." Every property in every market is categorized as an A, B, or C. Look at a few of each and you will quickly be able to determine on sight which building fits into which class.

UNDERSTANDING LEASES

You may wonder why I'm bringing up leases so soon; after all, you just began looking at properties. The reason is as simple: it's leasing that drives your cash flow, and cash flow is a significant definer of property value.

There are four kinds of leases. The type of leases that you have for your tenants will dictate the amount of involvement that you and your property managers will have maintaining and paying for upkeep to your properties. The decision to go with one lease or another depends on the market and what tenants are accustomed to paying in that market. In Chicago or New York, for example, it's "triple net" for office; on the West Coast it's "gross." Even within a single building there can be different tenants signed to different types of leases.

Here are the types of leases that are out there. Get to know them. We'll refer to them in the remainder of the book.

Gross: Gross means full service. You as property owner would pay for all utilities, upkeep, and maintenance. The tenant pays just the rent.

Net: This can mean a number of things, but generally it means the tenant pays for one or more aspects of the property's utilities, upkeep, and maintenance. For example, net-utilities means the tenant will pay for utilities. Net-janitorial means the tenant will pay for janitorial.

Triple Net: In this type of lease, the owner is responsible for structure, roof, parking, etc. The tenant covers all other expenses, including utilities, taxes, utility repair, maintenance, etc. Companies like Walgreens and Jack in the Box typically sign triple net leases. Triple net is designated NNN in the industry, and you'll see it often on sales literature.

Absolute Triple Net: Here, the tenant pays everything: real estate taxes, janitorial. If the roof caves in the tenant has to pay for it. This is the least amount of work for you, but you'll find these leases are typically in single-tenant buildings where the tenant almost owns the building. They are typically long-term leases and sometimes are what are known as "sale lease back" deals in which an owner/user sells the building to an investor and then leases it back for a long-term agreement.

Now Choose Your Passion

For me, I didn't want to get into residential, or hospitality, or strip retail, or any other area of commercial real estate because they were not of interest to me. I chose commercial office and I'm glad I did. It's something I liked and was at ease with; it put me face-to-face with community business leaders and provided a great foundation to network and become a part of the business community. It was just something I knew I'd enjoy.

What do you enjoy? Forget about the money for a minute. If everything were equal, what sector of real estate would you choose? This is your time to reflect and decide for good.

PREPARING FOR WEEK 3

In the week ahead, you'll need some serious study time set aside. You'll be poring over real estate properties on paper and online, learning the terms, understanding the differences, and recognizing what I call red and green flags—those things that signal "pass it up" or "possible opportunity." You won't be driving around like you did this week. Instead, you'll be taking virtual tours of properties on paper and online and getting down to the particulars. Make a pot of coffee and plan on a few late nights or early mornings.

CHAPTER 6

EXPLORING THE FUNDAMENTALS

WEEK 3 OF 9

I t's Week 3 of the nine-week program and you have already accomplished quite a bit. You've made some decisions about your real estate future, and you've taken one or more rides around your town jotting down both areas and properties of interest along with their key characteristics. You've realized by now that commercial real estate comes in many shapes and sizes.

The last chapter provided overviews of the real estate options, and, with the little extra time afforded in the last chapter for reflection, you should have decided two things: 1) the initial type of commercial real estate you want to pursue, and 2) the areas within your community that will become your focus. These are two very big decisions that are critical as we begin researching the fundamentals of the properties you've found that fit that bill—at least they look like they fit the bill, at this point. Time and some effort will tell.

You'll find this chapter to be helpful not because we will arrive at the one single property that you'll want to invest in, but because you'll learn how to rule out properties quickly. Learn this skill and you will save huge amounts of time. Let me put it this way, the better you get at understanding the fundamentals, the more free time you'll have to do other things. If I had to spend countless hours researching a property every time one interested me, I'd have time for nothing else. I know you're like me. Your time is valuable. That's probably why you're interested in owning commercial real estate in the first place. You want a little freedom to enjoy life.

In fact, as you learn how to assess a property by exploring the fundamentals, the skill itself will begin to feel like a sixth sense. By knowing the methods, and with enough practice, you'll be able to determine whether or not a property is worth a closer look, in a matter of minutes. The only question after that is, what *do* you plan to do with all your spare time?!

Reading and Understanding Offering Memorandums (OMs)

If you aren't talking to brokers yet, "OM" is short for offering memorandum. OMs let you compare the features, figures, and value of multiple properties that have actually sold to another investor, apples to apples, as they say. Imagine how difficult it would be to actually assess which property investment is best without tools that provide the information you need to quickly assess worth. It would be next to impossible.

The challenge is that not all OMs are the same and, unfortunately, not all of them contain the important information you need. Some contain the information but list it in a way that is different than other OMs. Actually, they are sales sheets prepared by brokers to sell a property, so yes, the rule here is buyer beware. There is no national or international standard for OMs. I've seen single-page OMs, multi-page OMs, OMs with a strong sales pitch, and OMs with just the data and a photo. They tend to be all over the board, and much of the information is superfluous at this stage of the game. This is where the knowledge, skill, and, eventually, instinct comes in. Great investors can pull the information they need from the OM quickly; good ones can't. Later, I'll reveal my Six Non-Negotiables, but we'll also go over what everything else on an OM means and how it plays into this process of elimination.

Understand that your goal from this point forward is to first understand the potential opportunity and then to minimize risk. Remember, real estate investing, like any investing, involves risk. The difference is that there are tools, and, as you'll see later, people and processes that minimize risk and give you the unfair advantage. As I said before, all I want in life is an unfair advantage. I won't compromise my ethics to get it; I don't have to, because in real estate investing, knowing more than the next person can give you the unfair advantage. It's a beautiful thing.

RESEARCHING THE MARKET— SEEING THE TRENDS

Thank goodness the real estate industry is loaded with research information and materials. The bad news is that the industry is loaded with research information and materials. It can be quite overwhelming. In this section of the book, I'm going to cut through the clutter and recommend the sources and the materials that are truly important. I definitely use CoStar.com, a website from the CoStar Group. You can also go to websites of large brokerage firms like CBRE and Cushman and Wakefield and others to do your research. Some require you to sign up or pay a monthly fee, or you can get your real estate broker to push the trend information your way. He or she certainly has it available. Once you start seeing the patterns, you'll learn to buy for tomorrow, not today. This is one of the most important concepts in this book.

RESEARCHING THE PROPERTY—
THE OM, DEMYSTIFIED

Now you know why I'm such a proponent of knowing your stuff and being smart. Having the unfair advantage can save you from mistakes and it can make you a lot of money. The OM is an important step on the road to getting smart. Let's review what an OM should contain.

As much as I'd like to say every OM has all the information you need, the truth is there isn't one that includes everything. Again, that's where working smart comes into play. Why waste time making calls for missing information, when a smart investor knows in the early research and analysis phase that there are only a few key things you really need to look for.

This exercise is not about deciding which property is best; it's about eliminating the ones that don't measure up. You can easily find OMs online by going to Loopnet.com or the Loopnet app, finding a property or two that you may want to learn more about, and contacting the listing broker. Some commercial brokerages will allow you to download the OM without contacting the agent first. They may just want your email address before you do so. CBRE is one of those brokers. We'll talk more about contacting brokers in a later chapter, so hold off on making the call for now.

Take a look at the list and the descriptions below. Read them all so you understand the importance and how they can help you add properties to your short list and eliminate ones that just aren't a fit with your goals and your situation.

EYE CANDY

Recognize that the listing broker is trying to sell you on the property and the goal is to make the property look and sound as appealing as possible. Smart investors don't fall for the sales pitch, but believe me, there's always something to learn.

Property Photo: Look for curb appeal, design of building, window line, and tenants. If the tenant seems like one who could be here today, gone tomorrow, I generally pass. If the design of the building is strange, I pass as well. If it's strange to me, it will be strange to prospective tenants and future buyers. I like flexible designs that have broad appeal.

Sales Description: Look to see if the size and price are within your parameters. If they're not in the ballpark, pass. By that I mean, if you're looking for a million-dollar property and this one is in the five-million range, it's a quick elimination.

Tenant Description: This is important. I want to know the tenant mix and know that they are reputable companies. I seldom take the broker's word for it. If the property makes it though this elimination round and into the "maybe" pile, I will investigate tenants further.

Investment Highlights: These are what the broker thinks are the big selling points. Again, this can be a good overview. What compels you to buy will also help you sell it someday.

Location Highlights: This can read like something written by the city's office of tourism, and, in fact, it probably was pulled from that kind of website. Where the property sits is helpful, but with experience, you'll know the property from the address. Is this within your location parameters? Is the access good? Do the adjacent streets back up during rush hour traffic? Can you find it? If you can't find it, the next buyer won't be able to find it either. True story: I have a building on a main street and we were constructing a second building in the office center that sits on the secondary side street. The city wanted the new building to have the secondary street address. I fought and paid to have the new building's address on the same street as the other buildings. It paid off; people were able to find the building and it's now leased.

By doing your parameter research up front, you can quickly see if your building fits your parameters. You can keep your buildings organized by product type, and then build your database in preparation for adding future properties. What you'll end up with is a building database and greatly expanded market knowledge.

GENERAL INFORMATION

This is valuable information because it helps you understand the building itself. There are a few very important pieces of data here that will not only help you know at a quick glance whether the property is in the running, but also if it matches your goal.

Broker Contact Information: Brokers are like knowledge banks. In the beginning, you can always learn something from them. If the building makes it into the running, you'll be contacting the broker.

Location Address: Also very important, the location address allows you to go online and visually see the property using Google Maps, Google Earth, or other free mapping software. You'll see what other properties are around it right from the maps online. If the property passes all the other tests, you may want to take a ride. Don't waste time and fuel now, though.

Building Size: I like knowing this right up front to ensure I'm in the right ballpark in terms of my goals and my finances.

Year of Construction: To me, this is important because I tend to invest in newer buildings, but even if you want to invest in older buildings, this is an important indicator of how much repair, improvements, ADA (Americans with Disabilities Act) compliance, asbestos potential, power availability, and city zoning/ordinance issues you will have.

Parking: This is a big one. If the ratio of parking spaces to building square footage is not in line, I pass on the property immediately. Know this standard for your city or town. Often, there is no room for expansion, and even if there is, parking lots cost a lot of money to build.

Property Taxes: To me, this is good to know, but not really important at this stage. Later, yes. Now, no.

Tax Parcel Number: This may come in handy should the property makes it to the "maybe" pile. You always want to verify all tax records, and this number allows you to do that.

Zoning: This is very important because if you are looking for a building to do one thing and the property you are considering is zoned for something else, keep looking. Rezoning hearings are expensive and are never sure unless you make your living through entitlement work.

Property Type: This is a description that will help you know if the property is within the parameters of your goal.

Builder: This is nice to know if the property makes it to the "maybe" pile. You'll want to know as much as you can about the construction, but not right now.

Construction Type: Also nice to know for later, but this is of little concern right now.

Improvements: "Improvements" is a term used to describe how the property—the land—has been improved with a building and infrastructure. It does not refer to improvements made to the building itself. This is simply an overview which can help you eliminate properties that don't meet your goal.

RENT ROLL

This section of the OM defines the nature and duration of the tenant leases. Some OMs have just the basics and others go into more detail. Following are all the lease information options that can show up on an OM:

Type: In the last chapter we talked about the types of leases—gross, net, triple net, and absolute triple net. That's what we mean by type. Lease type is good to know because it indicates the kinds of expenses the owner has and that you might be responsible for.

Term: "Term" refers to the duration of the lease(s) with the tenant(s). Long leases tend to be good because they are more secure, but in upward-trending markets, investors can miss out on escalating rents. Short leases are good because at the end of every lease is the opportunity to raise rents to the current market rate, but the down side is a lack of security. If you have decided you want more or less risk, lease term becomes a big issue. Generally, the longer the lease with credit-worthy tenants, the less risk.

Lease Commencement: This is when the lease started and gives you an idea of how many years are left and how long each tenant has been in the property. Like a resume with gaps in employment, it can bring to light gaps and inconsistencies in lease patterns. For instance, I toured the tenant spaces of a building I was considering and noticed that the OM showed one tenant had signed the lease in November. It was February and the space was vacant. That's a red flag; something's not right.

Lease Expiration: This is the scheduled expiration date and gives you a read on how long before you might be looking for a new tenant or how long you'll have to wait to raise rent.

Options to Renew: This indicates the tenant's renewal terms. An example is two five-year options, which means the lease options could run for ten more years with the same lease terms if they are fully exercised.

Expenses: This is a further explanation of lease type and confirms what expenses are paid by the tenant and what ones are paid by the owner.

Current Rents: These are very important because, at this stage of the game, you will want to know whether the rents for this building are competitive with the market. Combine that with the lease term and you start to get a picture of whether this property has the capacity to grow rents or is declining.

What you may be noticing is that this is a process of recognizing red and green flags: the little things that don't seem right or the little things that look like gems. Look at them with the objective of eliminating the properties that don't make sense.

Financial Information

Okay, now we're getting to the meat of this whole exercise. A great investor can gather almost everything he or she needs to know to establish a short list of properties from the financials on an OM. Let's go into each in a bit more detail.

Listed Sales Price: This is nice to know, but as you'll learn in this book, you'll calculate a fair sales price using the financial formulas that smart investors use. I never look at a sales price and think, "Too high. I'll negotiate the price down 15 percent." Commercial real estate doesn't work that way. Pricing is a function of the actual Net Operating Income (NOI), which is the money generated through rent and other operations, and the potential NOI. See how this is beginning to work? If the sales price is way far off from a reasonable market price determined by the NOI, that's a red flag. If I'm interested, I stay in touch with the owner, but take it no further for the time being. Later in this chapter, we'll go over how to do this quantitative analysis.

Price per Square Foot: This is a great number to glance at to see if the seller is being at all realistic compared to the market. If I see a building that is priced below replacement cost, that's a green flag, provided there is no functional obsolescence like too few parking spaces for the size of the building. You'll know how a building stacks up to the market based on comparables, which we'll discuss later in this chapter.

Net Operating Income: The net operating income (NOI) is defined as the gross operating income (GOI) of a property minus its operating expenses *(NOI = GOI - Expenses)*. Operating expenses are things like management costs, janitorial, maintenance, supplies, taxes, utilities, etc. In short, this number is an important variable you need to determine how much cash flow the property generates in a year and the cost to run the building. Why is this important? Because cash flow is what ultimately provides you financial freedom!

Debt: Is there existing debt? What is the amount? Is it assumable? Can it be paid off? If so, what is the cost to do so? Debt actually kills a lot of deals, but it makes some deals as well. When financing is hard to get, a building with good, assumable debt is a green flag. The red flag is a building with low leverage, non-assumable loans with a high pay-off at interest rates that are above market.

Down Payment: Not many OMs include how much money you must put down, but some do. This is only relevant on a building that has existing debt. If there is no debt on the building, then this number will come from the lender when you set up your own financing.

Debt Service: This number shows how you will pay down any debt. You might secure your own financing and have your own debt service schedule, but if that isn't the case, you'll need this number to calculate cash flow. If there is no existing debt on the building, again, this number will come from the lender.

Cash Flow: Here's why NOI and debt service are important. *Cash Flow = NOI - Debt Service*. Few OMs contain this number, but you can see how easy it is to calculate. This is a very important number, so consider this a basic introduction. We'll go into more detail in Chapter 9.

Capitalization Rate (Cap Rate): The cap rate shows the expected annual return percentage for a given property, much like a bond yield gives the expected rate of interest in a given year. If the information that is listed on the OM or that you gather is complete and accurate, then the cap rate will tell you if this is a good investment compared to the market, or not. If your information, particularly NOI—which is hard to calculate accurately—is incomplete or based on estimates, then the cap rate will be an estimated return.

The benefit of using cap rate when evaluating real estate investments is that you can determine the expected revenue from the investment and define what the investment is worth based on that revenue. No longer will you ever consider the listed sales price on the OM as anything more than a guide. Instead, you'll calculate the sales price using a simple cap rate investment formula. The cap rate calculation tells you instantly whether the investment will be profitable and whether it will meet your investment goals.

The beauty of cap rate is that it takes all the other important numbers into consideration, and for that reason, I can look at a cap rate on an OM and know within seconds what the real purchase price should be and whether the property warrants any further consideration. How do you know if the cap rate on the OM is valid? The number that is listed should equal the listed or derived *NOI ÷ Purchase Price*. Using simple math, you can calculate the price of the property using cap rate with the formula *Cap Rate x NOI*.

Cash on Cash: This is defined as the annual cash return on the annual cash invested. If you have the cash flow number (which is *NOI — Debt Service*), the price of the property (which is *Cap Rate x NOI*) and the debt service number you can calculate cash on cash. For example, if you invested $1 million in cash into a property in a given year, you financed the rest, and the property threw off $80,000 that year in cash flow, the cash on cash calculation would be 8 percent. It's a simple calculation to arrive at that percentage. The annual income divided by annual dollar investment equals cash on cash: $80,000÷$1,000,000=0.08.

ROI (Return on Investment): This value takes into account the NOI of a property, the asset value of the property, *and* the proceeds of the property after the property is sold. The difference between ROI and cap rate which you'll recall is an indicator of return based on just the investment amount and the NOI, is that this number takes into account the proceeds from the sale of the property.

IRR (Internal Rate of Return): This is the percentage rate earned on each dollar invested for each period it is invested. This number gives you another way to compare investments in terms of the investment's yield. Calculating IRR isn't as simple as some of the other values we've been discussing because it considers time and the present and future values of money. This is where your HP calculator comes in. Just use the function keys and the process of calculating IRR as you learned in the tutorials.

USING OMS—MY SIX NON-NEGOTIABLES TEST

By this point, you have probably looked at several OMs. Eventually, you will be able to look at them and know within a few minutes whether the property warrants any more of your time. You'll begin to see patterns. When I am considering a real estate investment, ruling out the ones I'm not interested in has become second nature. Over the years, I have arrived at my Six Non-Negotiables Test that I use every time. And most importantly, I stick to my guns! A building that fails even one aspect of this simple test is off my list.

Location: I don't care how amazing the building is, how many windows it has, or how wonderful the parking lot is, it absolutely must be in a location that I like. That means it must have upside potential in five to ten years. The building must be in an area that is increasing in value; it cannot be in a declining neighborhood or area of the city. The last thing I want to be is the pioneer going in to revitalize an area, and I certainly don't want to be an investor who is riding the slide down. Revitalization is fine for investors who specialize in those types of projects, or for very experienced investors who look to invest in challenged areas when the real estate cycle is at its peak and good moneymakers in prime locations are few and far between. That's not my thing; either the location is on the up, or I am out.

Functionally Sound: The parking lot must be an appropriate size for the occupancy of the building. There's nothing worse than owning a building that doesn't have adequate parking. Actually, there is one thing worse. It's owning a building that doesn't meet parking/occupancy requirements and not having the ability to increase parking lot size. I also will rule a property out if the look—meaning the architectural design—of the building is undesirable. After all, I am going to have to lease this building, and few businesses want to be in a building that doesn't represent them well. Buildings with good design but are in need of work are fine. It's the bad design I avoid. Then there are things like electrical capacity, asbestos, low ceilings, column spacing, lack of windows, etc. that are either impossible or very expensive to change and cause tenant prospects to keep looking. I always say, if the building or some aspect of it makes me not want to be there, it will have the same effect on others looking to rent. I go with my gut.

No Bad Debt: Some properties are seemingly perfect until you look at the debt on the building itself. Think of it as property that comes with baggage. I always look at this because I will disqualify a property with bad debt that cannot be paid off. An example of this is an industrial building that we were trying to buy. Everything looked really good until we discovered one problem: the building had a loan in place that didn't expire for ten more years. The interest rate was 3 percent higher than the going market. Additionally, this loan had no inexpensive pre-payment provision. This loan baggage completely lowered the value of this building.

No Escalating Land Leases: You think that when you own the building, you always own the land. Not so! Some buildings are actually sitting on land owned by someone else. While this isn't always a problem, if the land lease particulars include big future increases, I'm not interested. Why? Because if I have a terrific long-term tenant with an annual rent increase of a reasonable percentage, I'm pretty happy. If one day, my operating costs on the property escalate because my rent to the landholder increases, then my profitability declines. That's one scenario. Or I raise the rent accordingly and the tenant leaves because my rent is now too high for the market. That's another scenario. How about when I go to sell the building some day? The next buyer is either going to avoid high land lease properties or he is going to consider it and compare my building's operating performance to others without land lease issues. I'll probably lose. Escalating land leases can make a building harder to lease, keep leased, and market and sell in the future.

A Deal I Can't Buy "Right": As is often said about real estate, you make your money when you buy, not when you sell. When I'm considering properties, I keep my emotions and my ego out of it. As much as I would love to own a prestigious building on a high-visibility corner in the prime area of town, if I can't buy it right, I'm not going to do it. What does "buy it right" mean? It means many things, but first and foremost, the property must have positive cash flow and I must be able to get it below replacement cost.

Product Type or Building I Don't Understand: This comes down to specializing and staying within your niche. For me, that means I will not consider no-zoning properties, meaning properties that will require entitlement work. Working my way through town and city planning and zoning committees and town council hearings is not how I want to spend my time. It is labor intensive, costly, and not where I play. I also walk away from abstract, historic or urban revitalization because that is not what I do. Keep in mind, historic buildings may be your passion, so you will seek them out and avoid commercial high-rises, for example. That's fine. The point here is to stay within your specialty and not get drawn into that wonderful Victorian home-turned-office in a historic district of town if you don't know what you're doing in that niche. Likewise, if Victorian is your thing, walk away from that mini-warehouse that's supposedly "a steal."

Putting It All Together

So there you have it. A walk through an OM, and within it, a lot of important formulas that help you determine a property's value. A good thing to do at this point would be to take each one of these formulas and copy them onto a cheat sheet that you can keep handy as a reference. Be sure to list the formula itself along with the formula's relevance.

Additionally, go to the Internet and find as many OMs in your area as you can and begin taking a look at them just for practice. Print them out and mark any and all green flags and red flags you see on a given property. Be sure to eliminate anything that doesn't meet my Six Non-Negotiables. Practice will give you the instinct you need to really succeed in this part of the business, and it is a crucial part of the business, to be sure.

As you are working through the OM exercise, keep them organized on your computer, in files, whatever is easy for you, but keep them organized by location and property type. This is the beginning of your market intelligence file. Buildings seldom go away, as you know, so the information you collect today is just the start of that property's permanent record. Viewed together over time, all the properties—including their current status and their history—paint a vivid portrait of where the market is going. Combine that with your knowledge about the neighborhood, demographics, and the real estate cycle and you have a multi-dimensional picture of the past, present, and even the future.

Preparing for Weeks 4 and 5

In the coming weeks, you'll be spending more time evaluating properties from the comfort of your own office or home. That means another pot of coffee and a few more late nights or early mornings. In addition to that, you'll also be out in the world meeting and talking to people in the industry. Free up some time during the next two work weeks for appointments and meetings. This is your debut as a real estate investor, so get mentally prepared. Confidence is everything, as is asking a lot of questions. Welcome to my world!

CHAPTER 7

ADVANCED RESEARCH

WEEKS 4 AND 5 OF 9

Welcome to weeks 4 and 5. So far, if you've been following the nine-week program in this book, you've attained a good idea of what your market looks like. You've selected the type of properties that most interest you, and in the last chapter, you learned how to read property , what the terms mean, and how to decipher the important information from the hype. The purpose of all this is to help you perform the difficult work of narrowing your choices—commercial real estate is such a big industry that you really must choose. Another important purpose in all this is simply to educate you and prepare you for talking with others in the profession.

Everyone likes to appear knowledgeable and intelligent when talking with people in business. It's human nature. I want you to be prepared because, right out of the gate, you need to be taken seriously by others in the profession. I recognize you might be a little apprehensive. People in my profession talk and word gets around. It's actually a pretty small community, and no one wants to be the person who asks the stupid question and never lives it down.

As a commercial broker, I've actually taken calls from people who ask the most naïve questions. I get calls all the time from people who will say they want to buy a parcel of land for $3 a foot when I have it in escrow for $23 per square foot. I tell them that and then they say, "Oh, thanks," and hang up. I'll never take another call from that person. I've taken too many of those calls and the outcome is never good. They waste a lot of time.

Here are examples of questions that signal "rookie": Inappropriate use of questions are big. "I'm looking for some warehouse space in an office building." "I need 2,000 square feet in XYZ building"—and that building only has 10,000-square-foot tenants. Some people call totally uninformed about the market. They'll say they want space in a Class A building and want to pay $15 a foot when the building leases for no less than $30 a foot. I know from just ten seconds on the phone with people like this that they are either not serious or not informed, or both. I prefer to work with seasoned investors, but I know there are brokers out there who prey on the uninformed. There are less-than-ethical people in every walk of life. Know that most people are aboveboard, but just the same, you want to be prepared and professional so you don't get taken for a ride. Here's how you get that way.

MAKE THE EASY CONTACTS FIRST

When I was in college, a career counselor told me to never call the recruiter for your dream job first. Call that person last once you are warmed up and seasoned. She was right, and I'm going to give you the same advice here. Make the easy calls and take the low-stress meetings first. For example, rather than call the top commercial broker in your market to get a feel for a neighborhood or a building, do your own research.

A great first step is simply get out and meet the people. Walk into a building you like. Talk to a few tenants in the area. Meet with building managers, the cleaning crews, people who live and work in the area. Walk into the Starbucks nearby—chances are there are at least two or three—and see what the clientele is like. Ask the baristas what they like about working in the area. What they don't like. Stop in at all hours—before work, during work, at lunch, in the afternoon, and especially the evening. Check out the local convenience store, the restaurants, and the nightclubs. I've seen areas completely transform from wonderful workplace by day to downright dangerous at night. It happens, and those kinds of drastic swings in environment can severely impact your ability to get tenants. Who wants to work in an area that becomes a crime risk after dark?

BACK UP YOUR GUT WITH DATA

Once you have your gut feeling from talking with people and hanging around the area at different times of day, back up what you are feeling with hard data. Traffic reports, crime rate reports, business growth, business failures and demographics, home values and raw land values are very important. Obviously, if the crime rate is up and home values are trending down, that's a bad sign. You never want to be in a declining area. As I've said before, there's no need for that. Even if your goal is to revitalize urban areas, there's no need to be the first one on the block. You should see positive trends before investing.

All this information is available online or through your local city or town government offices. It is not hard to find. Even though you may think that your visual assessment is enough, avoid the temptation to skip the data step. Yes, it takes extra time, but it may reveal something that you would have missed otherwise.

This information is critical and well worth taking time to review. Equally important, if not more important, is a review of comparable commercial properties in the area. Also known in the industry as "comps," this information gives you the idea of a property's value by equating or comparing it to what others have paid for similar properties in the area. While this kind of comparison shopping is helpful, no two commercial properties are equal. I typically consider those comps of properties that are most like the property I am interested in more reliable than the comps of properties that are really different.

The key is to find properties in your target area that have sold recently under open market conditions. You find these property records through paid services like CoStar Comps or online through LoopNet. com. You can pull comps together for free through your county assessor records of all properties. Those are online, too. All it takes is the parcel number or the street address. Comps are most effective when there have been a number of recent sales in the area. That activity gives you a better chance of finding a building or two that are very similar to the ones you are considering in your "maybe" pile.

Here's what a typical comp report looks like:

BUILDING DESCRIPTION

Deer Valley Business Center is a 48,082 square foot building including a 16,000 square foot mezzanine capability. The building is comprised of tilt concrete construction, steel reinforcement and extensive glass. The clear height is 24 feet and there are 238 total parking stalls.

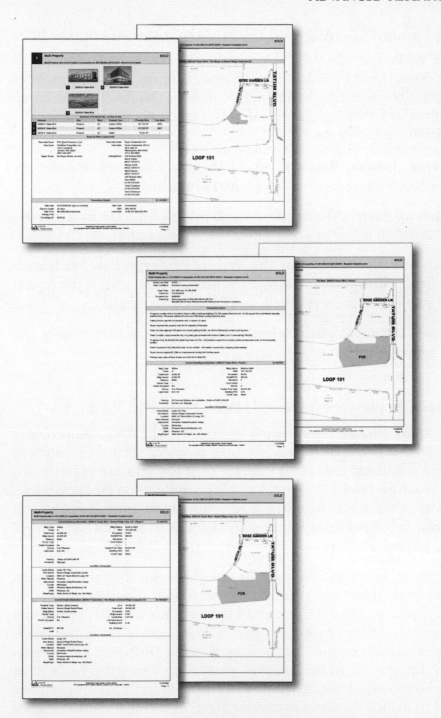

GET COMFORTABLE WITH FINANCIAL INFORMATION

This is also the time to do some research related to financing and to get comfortable with the financial aspects of the kind of properties you are considering. For example, contact a few lenders and set up exploratory meetings. The goal of the meetings is to discover the following information:

Current Interest Rates: What are the prime interest rate and the bank rates for commercial property investment?

Projected Interest Rates: How much or how little are interest rates expected to rise or decline in the coming quarter?

Loan-to-Value Amount for This Type of Property: How much is the bank willing to loan based on projected value, what is the typical amount of equity required, and the loan payments?

Fees: What are the loan origination fees for this kind of property, the property taxes, and insurance?

CHECK UP ON YOUR INVESTOR PROSPECTS

If you are considering bringing investors to the deal, you probably have a few in mind. Now is the time to check the backgrounds of those who have expressed interest or those you are planning to approach for capital. You may feel this is a little bit on the sneaky side, but don't think that way. This is what any smart professional person would do before getting into business with a partner, and these people will be your partners.

Of course, the first thing to do is a Google search. This will tell you a great deal about your partner prospects. Even if nothing shows up when you type their names and hit enter, that tells you something about them. Beyond Google, you can do a Dunn & Bradstreet credit report on each person's business by going to DnB.com. From there, you simply enter in the company name, city, and state. You will be able to buy reports of varying depth and complexity on the company and its principals. You can check references through mutual friends and colleagues and find out how they "behaved" with past investments. Are they the kind of investors who call every five minutes with a lot of questions, do they trust the experts and let them do their jobs, or are they somewhere in between?

Also understand that checking up on a person is a two-way street. Once you approach someone with a deal, that person is very likely to check up on you, too. At least the smart investors will. So prepare yourself for that by having your credit in order and your reputation well established. I know the latter isn't something you do overnight, but if you've had some challenges in the past, the way you begin repairing a reputation is by starting this very moment.

GET TO KNOW YOUR PREFERRED PROPERTY TYPE…INTIMATELY

Now is the time to begin your journey to becoming an expert in your preferred property type. If you're like me and prefer office buildings, then completely immerse yourself in the field. If it's mini-storage, then dive in head first. How do you do that? I started by looking up every possible article in papers like your local *Business Journal*, daily newspaper, or local business magazines. You can do this online and source the archives. Look for all the news related to development and property of your type in geographic areas of interest.

Begin building a database of buildings. Even ones that aren't available now may be available at a later time. I have a database of the fifty-five buildings in Phoenix that I want to own. I keep tabs on them and the neighborhoods they are in. When the time is right, I will make my move, but I couldn't do that if I hadn't done the upfront work well in advance of the opportunity. You'll find that as you become familiar with your property type and your preferred locations, there will be buildings and locations that you would love to own. That's good! When the time is right and with the proper amount of knowledge, you'll be in a position to act.

As you continue to read up on your property type and market and learn more about real estate in general, you'll find people in the business speak a language all their own. Get to know the lingo. There are a number of real estate glossaries online with many of the most commonly used terms in commercial real estate. One I particularly like is InvestorWords.com. You'll also pick up words and phrases from those whom you meet. While you can't fake your way to sounding like you know what you're talking about simply by knowing the language, you can come across as more professional and with credible. Simply put, you want to understand what people are telling you, know what you're talking about, and talk like you know it, too.

KEY CONTACTS ON YOUR SIDE

We live in a very interdependent world. I can't think of anything that we do without the help of other people. Even the most simple tasks we do in our day we don't do alone. Take brushing our teeth for example. It took countless numbers of people to design and manufacture the toothbrush and toothpaste. Eating a sandwich for lunch took a team, too: people planted and grew the grain, milled it, shipped it, and eventually baked the bread. Even writing this book has taken hundreds of people throughout my career to shape my learning and my business so I could share this with you.

Here are the people you will want to have on your team and with whom you will want to begin developing solid relationships. They will help you time and time again, not just with matters in their areas of expertise, but with your work in general. These people will become part of your extended organization and they will provide you with knowledge, insider tips, and trends. You help them; they help you.

Lenders: Visit several lenders and get to know them. It's always good to have more than one source of capital, but what you'll find is that you'll connect with one or two lenders better than the others. Not just in the sense of personality fit, but in terms of the projects they prefer to finance. Ask them specific questions. For example, if you are interested in mini-storage properties, be very up-front with questions like these:

- Do you fund mini-storage properties at this given amount?

- Can you give me a list of the people whose projects you have funded so that I may call them?

- You haven't done mini-storage projects; can you give me the names of lenders who do?

- Who are your biggest competitors in this area?

- What kind of activity have you seen in mini-storage lately?

- What's your opinion of the outlook?

You can see why it is important to have your interests narrowed down. You want to ask the right questions, not a million questions. In the course of asking these questions, you are growing your network—which in this business is critical to success.

Understand also that in commercial real estate, unlike residential, lenders are not always banks. In fact, they most likely are *not* banks; often the lenders are institutions like insurance companies, capital companies, or other types of companies that raise and lend large sums of money. So how do you find these companies and contact them? That happens through your bank—simply ask who else lends money for this kind of project. They say your lender is never your friend, but in this case, a lender that provides you such valuable networking contacts is a friend indeed. One lead leads to the next.

Mortgage Brokers: Mortgage brokers will be a tremendous resource to you. Ask if they do or have done the kind of deals you are targeting. They will also be able to tell you other sources of capital. The question you want to ask here is, "Who do you correspond for?" In essence, mortgage brokers are "finders" for companies with money to invest in commercial property. Your mortgage broker will help you put together your package, which includes all the particulars about the property, the amount of equity, the amount of the loan, the interest rate, the mortgage amount, payments, etc. Then they can connect you with lenders that will be interested in such a deal.

Commercial Real Estate Appraisers: When forming relationships with appraisers, I ask all the same questions I asked lenders regarding area of specialty, competition, and level of interest in my deals. I do this until I have established relationships with the ones I know will work hard for me. Until I know that the appraiser is qualified, I comparison shop a bit. In this case, I'm looking for competence, and the only way you, as a novice, will be able to make a good judgment of competence is to compare the work of a few appraisers.

I always ask for samples of their work. I find out who does their research. Then I make a point of getting to know that person. I take the researcher to lunch. No one ever takes these people to lunch and the results for me are always eye opening. After all, this is a person who spends his or her days studying your market and its trends. Just ask and they'll share with you how they do their comps, where they get their information, what their outlook is and more. It will be well worth the cost of a sandwich and an hour of your time.

Environmental Professionals: You may be thinking, "Why would I want to talk to people who check buildings for environmental issues so early? Why not wait until I actually have a building to show them?" The fact is, the more you know up front about the environmental issues that property owners face, the better off you'll be. In fact, the more you know about environmental concerns, the better you will be able to eyeball a property and see the flags that signal big dollars in remediation. They can also provide ballpark estimates of how much remediation can cost.

I've known lots of people who lost money on their first deal because they didn't know how to look for "functional obsolescence"—outdated features that can't easily be changed—in buildings. Certainly you've heard of things like asbestos, lead paint, and ADA requirements. Buildings must comply with federal, state, and local laws that apply to these issues. Mold is another concern, and your "Phase 1" environmental contact can educate you on all these kinds of things and more.

City codes change all the time. Classic design, classic functionality, is what I look for; I don't buy buildings with inherent problems. The trend is for sustained development that involves renewable materials, alternative energy, and the use of recycled local sustainable products. Green building and Leeds certification are worth knowing, and your contacts can help you and guide you through this new terrain. This all has marketability advantages as environmental progress marches forward. Just like the technology advances in medicine, information technology, and everything else in our world, building technology is changing, too.

Other Friends in Your Network: By now, you get the idea that your mission is to contact these people, ask them questions, and get to know them, their expertise, their competitors and their industries. The process is the same, the questions, the answers and the learning are all that differ. Here are the other kinds of friends you want to have in your network. The cool part is that over time, many of these people will become your actual friends:

- Surveyors
- Property Inspectors
- Contractors
- Property Managers
- Property Brokers
- Contract Attorneys
- Leasing Attorneys
- Accountants
- Financial Analysts
- Tax Appeals/ Abatement Specialists
- Investors

This is your time to really do your advanced research. It's not the kind of research that comes primarily from the Internet or from books. It's the kind of research that comes from people smarter than yourself. It's important at this point to understand that the only way to succeed in this business is to realize that you need people with more experience, more knowledge, and more contacts to help you. There is so much to learn from them!

Too many people let ego get in the way and miss this important, critical step because they are afraid of looking stupid. If you follow the nine-week program in this book, you won't look stupid. Rather, you will come across as a person who, wisely, is learning as much as he or she possibly can from others. You will be viewed as new, but smart for doing things the right way.

Preparing for Week 6

Week 6 will be a learning week and an overflow week. Continue your appointments and continue developing your network by meeting with the right people and asking the right questions. You can also begin working on some legal paperwork that will be required for any deal that you do. You'll also want to make sure you have taken a new look at your "maybe," your "yes" and your "no" piles of properties in light of your new knowledge from your meetings. Make the necessary adjustments because, in Week 6, you'll get a solid picture of the money side of things.

CHAPTER 8

FIND THE MONEY

WEEK 6 OF 9

At last! Here it is Week 6 and we're going to talk money. You have been wondering how long before money enters the picture, and now is the perfect time to delve deeply into the subject. After all, in the goal-setting chapter, you already took a look at your finances and put together a rough idea of what kind of money you have available and what you are willing to invest. Now is the time to talk about how to put that money to use and actually raise more if needed.

I started my real estate investing career as a limited partner investing in other people's deals. I still have a few investment groups that I invest with today. The way I see it, I don't corner the market on good deals. Even though, or maybe because, I was in the business, I started out investing in other people's deals. I sought out what I considered the best three groups in my market and invested $25,000 with each one. I looked to see how they analyzed deals, what their deal flow was like, how they communicated with me, and how they treated the property asset—in general, the pros and cons of each group. What I found was that each group had its own strengths. One group I did only one deal with, not because they weren't successful, but because I didn't like the way they operated. Another got too big for me, and a third I still invest with today.

I actually participated in several deals as a limited partner before ever leading one as a managing partner. How did I know I was ready? When I could see things that I would have done differently, and, in my opinion, better than the managing partner of those deals. Once I could see the opportunities others missed, I knew with confidence that I could take on a bigger deal than simply a building that I purchased on my own.

Some people who invest in commercial real estate actually never move beyond the limited partner phase, and there is nothing wrong with that. They may have other businesses that they run and don't have the time or the desire to manage deals. They may find the returns they get through a limited partner arrangement work for them. They enjoy the income and the freedom of not having to put in the sweat equity.

No matter which way you decide to focus your efforts—on either creating the deals or participating in them—this book will make you a smarter, more critical evaluator of opportunities, whether they be your own or someone else's.

A Lot, a Little, or Somewhere In-Between?

First-time real estate investors often wonder how much money it will take to invest in a commercial building. That's a question that isn't easy to answer. There are so many factors involved, including the kind of property you are looking at, size, location, comps in the area, how much cash you have on hand, and how much you can borrow. Actually, a better question is, "How much leverage do I want to have or will my lender allow me to have in my building?"

"Leverage" is a term used to define the use of borrowed capital to purchase an investment. Most people prefer to buy real estate using borrowed funds, or leverage, because there are a number of benefits to financing and because real estate investments are long-term. Also, why use your own cash when you can use someone else's to earn a good return?

Leverage allows you to invest in a property that you otherwise would not be able to touch. It enables you to purchase a higher value property using debt plus your own equity that you otherwise could not have afforded. When you use leverage, you can retain your capital for other investment uses such as purchasing a second building. You may be thinking one building would be a good start and probably enough, but think about it. Buying two buildings spreads your risk and offers you a hedge.

Robert Kiyosaki, in many of his books, talks about the difference between good debt and bad debt. Bad debt is the kind I hope you don't have. That includes high balances on credit cards, car loans, boat loans, a financed vacation, or any other *expense* you are paying off over time. And I do mean *expense*. Good debt, by contrast, is the debt you have on assets that generate cash flow. Assets are the opposite of expenses; they add value to your financial balance sheet and make you money, whereas expenses drain money. The goal is to acquire assets that pay you money and minimize expenses that drain it. Pretty logical when you think about it.

Leverage happens through real estate loans, which can take many forms, depending on who is lending the money, what the money is for, and who the borrower is. Market conditions certainly play a role, too. Let's go into a bit more detail about loans.

THE LANGUAGE OF LOANS

While all loans can be different, they all contain the same components:

Loan Amount: This is the amount of the purchase price that is funded through financing. When you hear people say a building is 75 percent leveraged, they mean that the lender has loaned 75 percent of the purchase price to the borrower. The borrower has 25 percent equity in the property, meaning the borrower has invested 25 percent of the purchase price. The amount a lender is willing to loan is based on that institution's underwriting rules, and every lender is different. Once you have the loan, the loan amount is also known as the "principle."

Interest Rate: This is the written interest rate that is used to calculate your loan payments. Interest rates can be fixed, meaning they do not go up or down during the life of the loan, or variable, meaning they fluctuate with some pre-determined market valuation, like treasury notes.

Loan Term: This term defines the length or duration of the loan. A loan term of 30 years means you must have the loan fully paid in that time. There is short- and long-term financing available today. Short-term is typically five years or less, and long-term is six years or more. The end of the loan term is called the maturity date.

Payment: This is how much money you'll pay on the loan every month. It's calculated using the initial loan amount, the interest rate, and the number of payments in the loan term.

Amortization: This is defined as the full amount you owe the lender and includes the loan amount plus the interest on that amount. The amortization period can be the same length as the loan term or it can be longer. There are different types of amortized loans:

- *Fully amortized:* In this type of loan, the loan term and the amortization term are the same. With this kind of loan, when you reach the end of the term, your loan amount is fully paid.

- *Partially amortized:* In this type of loan, the amortization period is longer than the loan term. With a partially amortized loan, at the end of the loan term, the loan is not completely paid off. You've heard of the term "balloon payment"? That's the remainder of the loan you owe (plus your last payment) at the end of the loan term. Payments are lower with this loan when compared to a fully amortized loan because the loan amount is amortized over a period longer than the loan term.

- *Non-amortized interest only:* In this type of loan, the payments equal only the interest due on the loan. In other words, your payment covers none of the loan principle. Because of that, at the end of the loan term, you'll still owe the full loan amount. Again, with this loan, payments are much lower compared to payments on fully or partially amortized loans because they cover only interest and none of the principle. This is the kind of loan that can get an inexperienced investor into trouble. They serve their purpose given the right exit strategy, but without a solid strategy, this loan type can be dangerous.

- *Negative leverage:* This means that your payments cover only a portion of the interest due on the loan and none of the principle or loan amount. The interest not paid accrues and compounds, so at the end of the loan term, you owe the unpaid interest (with accrued interest) plus the original loan amount. With this loan, you owe more than the initial loan amount at maturity. These loans have the lowest payments of all the loan types.

In my business, I stay away from negative leverage loans. Taking on debt allows you to leverage your investment, which is a good thing. You don't want to over leverage by taking on too much debt to make the numbers work on a property. You only want to leverage positively, meaning that your return is greater after the debt is in place than if there was no debt on the investment. For example, I just looked at a deal recently where the yield, or income return on investment, was 6.5 percent on a cash basis and I couldn't get a loan for less than 7 percent. That deal would have left me half a percentage point in the red. When you have negative leverage, you are taking on debt and getting no positive cash flow in return. You are banking on appreciation and putting money into the property along the way. For some people that's okay, but if I can't make money along the way, I'm not interested.

Each property will bring different types of loans. I might have to go to fifteen lenders to finally get the loan I need based on what I want the property to achieve. Most of my properties have been funded with loans. I use the lender's money to set up the deal, then, as the property's performance—meaning operating income—improves and the value goes up, I refinance and use the equity gain to either pay down the loan or invest tax free in another investment. If I use it to pay down the loan, then my loan payments go down, which improves my cash flow. My decision to take the cash or add another property to my portfolio is dependent on my goals and the market.

Loan Balance: This is the amount of principle you still owe at any given time during the loan term. Early in the loan, in a fully amortized loan, you'll have a higher loan balance than you will near the end of the loan term. With a non-amortized interest-only loan, your loan balance will be the same at the beginning and at the end of the loan term. With a negatively amortized loan, your loan balance will be higher at the end.

LET'S TALK ABOUT DEBT

Debt allows a small investor to go out and buy a bigger property. Financing helps leverage the money you have and make you more money faster than if you tried to grow with your own money alone. The dark side of debt is that you are borrowing money against an asset that you own or one that you are trying to buy and you will have to pay it back. Debt is to be used judiciously. People who use debt well can control more real estate that those who don't. In other words, debt used wisely allows them to own more properties and bigger properties.

So what does using debt wisely mean? First of all, as Robert Kiyosaki says, debt must be good debt—meaning debt that pays a return. An example is real estate. Bad debt is an expense like taking out a home equity loan to buy a pair of jet skis. Second, using debt wisely also means getting the right loan amount at the right terms for the specific investment. It doesn't mean getting the most debt that you can with lousy terms, and it doesn't mean taking anything you can get. What it means is looking at each individual investment and determining what your options are and what your risk tolerance is, and matching your risk, your tolerance, and your return. The best way to clarify this concept is through examples:

Your Own Building: For many people, their first real estate investments are buildings that will house their own businesses. Here, the most important thing to look at is what your debt payment will be. If your debt payment is close to or lower than your current lease payment as a renter, then the decision is easy. The building purchase makes sense. The tax benefits of owning a building are the icing on the cake. So, your assumption of debt— meaning the amount, the terms, and the guarantees—is based on the amount you and your business can afford to pay in rent on a monthly basis. Seek financing that fits your requirement, and keep searching even if you have to talk to fifteen different lenders, like I have in the past.

Building as Investment: When buying a building with other tenants already in place, what you need to consider is the stability of your cash flow to offset your debt payments. I like to make sure that the money coming in from operations, such as rent, cover the loan payment with a good cushion. I see people get in trouble because they don't have that cushion and then the unexpected happens— they lose a tenant—and they have to come up with the extra cash to cover the loan. If you have investment partners, that might mean making cash calls monthly to cover the loan payments. But if you don't have the cash to cover the loan, everyone—you and your investors, if you have them—can potentially lose the whole investment. I look at it simply: What do I need in terms of a loan so that I can sleep at night? I don't like being over leveraged and praying that all my tenants stay in business and can keep paying me rent. But I don't like to be under-leveraged either because that means too much of my cash is tied up in one building and I don't have enough to buy my next investment.

Undeveloped Land Investment: This is tricky because there is no income on undeveloped land. Unless I have a planned exit strategy in the next twelve to twenty-four months, I like to have as little debt on land as possible. Some land we have no debt on and others a little, but the last thing I want to do is feed huge sums of money to a land investment every month that isn't providing any cash flow. I know the asset is appreciating in value, but that's not enough for me to want to dole out thousands monthly.

Overleveraging is not good in real estate because real estate is cyclical. When the down cycles come, you want to have some buffer. But how much buffer is enough and how much is too much? The majority of the time, this will be limited by your lending sources because they have an interest in your investment working and you staying solvent, too. The question isn't one of enough, it's a question of enough for my risk tolerance.

For example, a lender may give you $750,000 on a $1 million investment. You may feel good about this amount of debt given your financial situation and the investment circumstances, or you may not. The point is, understand the relationship between debt service and operating income and know that if the latter doesn't cover the former, it is cash out of your and your investors' pockets each and every month.

I've had to make cash calls to my investors. They are not fun for me to make and they are not fun for my investors to get. Your investor has to write you a check on the spot and may have to do so every month until operating revenue once again covers the loan amount. This is a great way to lose investors for your next deal along with family and friends. It's a great way to make Thanksgiving and Easter very uncomfortable. Making cash calls is not how I like to spend my time. Early in my career, I met a guy who owned three million square feet of industrial space in a major metropolitan area free and clear. I can tell you he slept well at night and enjoyed cash flow monthly.

MONEY SOURCES

Now that you understand the language of loans and debt, let's talk about the different ways you can find money. As I mentioned earlier, when it comes to commercial real estate, loans don't always come from a bank. In fact, more often than not on big projects, they come from everywhere *but* banks.

Institutions are big sources of capital and they include insurance companies, pension funds, etc. These lenders have funds coming in through premiums in the case of insurance companies and retirement monies in terms of pension funds, and they need to invest it. Some of that money goes into real estate. Typically, institutions are interested in bigger deals and have $5 million to $20 million minimums. More typical for me, and you as you are starting out, are investment deals using banks or mortgage brokers who will match your investment with the right lender.

I also raise private money for the equity portion on all of my investments. This may sound like something that is far beyond the reach of anyone just starting out, and it may be challenging on your first deal. You'll quickly find that there are people out there, lots of them in your own backyard, who are looking for good places to put their money. As I mentioned earlier, I participate as an investor in others' deals that I think can bear fruit. Lots of private commercial real estate is funded this way. In fact, the bigger the deal, the more likely that there will be multiple investors owning portions of buildings. It's a way to spread risk and to hedge against downturns or unexpected occurrences in any one investment; a way to buy bigger properties than you would otherwise be unable to afford; and a way to bring in players with other areas of expertise that can help with managing, leasing, financing, raising equity, and even the legal aspects of real estate.

When you're just starting out, investing in more than one building immediately may be difficult. It can take time, and that's okay. I've been investing for almost twenty years, but when I first started out, I only bought a building here and there. There have been some years when I didn't buy anything because the market was bad—meaning the market was flying high. Today, I'm diversified in numerous holdings. Your future begins, however, with your first move in the here and now. That's what's important, and when it comes to money, you can go a few different ways:

Going Solo: If you decide you'd rather not take on partners and would rather limit your investment to your own financial resources, that's fine if it fits your goals as an investor. For example, owning a building alone is an ideal choice if the building is for your own business, or if you are looking for a smaller commercial property. There are lots of great $100,000 opportunities out there that are worthwhile as investments. All you'd need is about $25,000 to get in, and you finance the rest.

Look for older buildings in good condition with no functional obsolescence that have excellent tenants. Think of it this way, there's nothing wrong with a lower-end property that a well-respected local electrician "in business since 1995" calls home. If that electrician has a son or daughter working in the business, all the better. You have to love a long-term, successful tenant with a succession plan! I'm never snobbish about properties. If it fits my goals and the location, building, economics, and the outlook are right, then nothing is beneath me. Going solo, however, means your investment is limited by your own financial resources and position.

Taking on Partners: I've never funded a commercial real estate investment with 100 percent of my own money; I've always had partners. I like the idea that I can have more diversification and that I can leverage my own financial resources across several investments. Sometimes, no matter how you try to crunch the numbers, you just won't be able to go it alone, even though you want to. You'll need partners or investors to come in on the deal, and you may be thinking that means you'll be spending your time selling. (I knew there was a catch to this real estate thing!)

The truth is, a good real estate deal requires little selling. People are looking for ways to grow their money that makes sense. The key is making sure you truly have a good deal—and this book and your effort toward personal growth and team building will help with that. Another key is believing in your deal enough to put your own money in it. I do not invest in any deals where the managing partner—the person putting the deal together—has not invested his or her own money.

We'll get into more detail on deals later in this chapter, but knowing how deals are structured and participating in them are two different things. As I mentioned earlier, I participated in a few deals to learn my way around. Before I chose a deal to get in on, I met with several people who were looking for money to learn how they structure deals. I did this to compare; I wanted to see how many different paths there were. To be honest, in some cases I had no real interest in the investment itself, my meetings were learning ventures. My thinking was, I might get surprised with a solid investment, but if not, that was okay. My priority was to find a solid model that I could use to develop partnerships of my own. When you explore others' deals, they must disclose the particulars of ownership, including who is due what.

Lining Up Financing: They say to ask a bank for money when you don't need it, so that you'll have it set up when you do. That is true. The most important reason to have your financing all lined up in advance of any deal is so that you can move on an opportunity when you find one and so the seller knows you are serious. In the world of commercial real estate, most sellers are only interested in talking with people who have money—through equity investors, banks, institutions, etc.—virtually in hand. In the last chapter, which covered weeks 4 and 5 in the nine-week program, you should have met with several lenders and have a good idea of who you'd prefer to work with on your first deal. The time is now to pull the trigger with one (or more) of them to line up your financing. Like I said before, if the first one can't give you what you want, move on to the next.

CHAPTER 8

THE LAST WORD ON LEVERAGE

Leverage is one of the most amazing aspects of real estate. It's where you can use other people's money to generate a return on investment. Before you think this is like free candy in a candy store, just know what kind of leverage you can get. There are two sides of the coin on leverage. You can use other people's money to finance your investment if you are buying right and you are buying in the right time in the cycle and you have a cushion in your cash flow. That sounds pretty good. Yet it's not so good—the other side of the coin—if cash flows drop 20 percent like they did in 2008. Then leverage, or should I say poorly managed leverage, is not your friend.

When you have leverage it means you have payments, and with those payments comes interest, which is an unyielding master. When you take a loan, you have commitments every month, no matter whether or not you have a tenant, whether or not the tenant is paying you rent or paying you enough rent to cover the loan and other expenses. No matter what, you still have those payments. The crash of 2008 was due largely to over-leveraging. People over-borrowed and then, when the real estate cycle began its inevitable progression from Phase 2 to Phase 3, lots of people got into trouble.

I like to make sure I have prudent amounts of leverage. What is prudent? It depends on the investment. If I have a single tenant building, I like to have a year's safety net set aside in the event the tenant vacates. That means I can pay the loan and interest for an entire year from reserves if I have to until we find a new tenant. With a multitenant apartment building, for example, and 95 percent occupancy, if a few tenants move out it won't kill you, so you don't need as high of reserves. Many investors think the that it is different when they have big tenants like Starbucks or Walgreens, that the building will never go vacant. They can go vacant and they do; in 2008, many big retailers shut down hundreds of locations as consumer spending slowed. You may feel more secure with one big, highly accredited tenant, but you're actually more secure when you have many tenants.

The good news is that, today, it's hard to get over-leveraged because the banks are not loaning like they used to. They've taken their lumps as well, so they are smarter, too. To me, the best move is prudent amounts of leverage—which is the amount you think is prudent plus five to ten percent of that in additional reserves. It's all about cushion.

FINANCING THROUGH PARTNERSHIP STRUCTURES

One of the biggest hurdles new real estate investors have—at least in their minds—is learning how to set up partnerships. It starts to sound complicated with expensive attorneys involved, and contracts and negotiation points. These things make most people very uncomfortable at first, but once you get through your first investment and understand how real estate deals work, you'll find they are not scary at all. To familiarize you, here are the steps:

Set Up Your LLC: "LLC" stands for limited liability company, and every property investment you make should be set up in a unique company. There are many reasons for this, but the most critical one is for your own protection. Should a person get injured, for instance, in your building and sue you, he or she cannot sue for any of your personal assets or any of your other corporate assets. That person can only sue the LLC and its assets. Your tax attorney and accountant can share with you the many other important financial reasons for setting up LLCs for each property, but for now, understand this is how deals are done, regardless of whether you arc securing your equity capital from a bank, an institution, friends and family, or private equity partners.

Setting up an LLC is as easy as calling your attorney and spending a few hundred dollars to have it done. For good information, I suggest visiting corporatedirect.com. Here are the steps:

1. Have your LLC Articles of Organization prepared. Select your business name that is unique and does not contain any of the off-limit words like "finance," "trust," "city," etc. Your state will have a list. You must also end the company name with the designator "LLC."

2. Make sure your attorney prepares your Operating Agreement and minutes of meeting. These are crucial for protecting your limited liability entity.

3. Publish the notices in the local newspaper if you live in Arizona and New York; if you live anywhere else, check with your state to see if it is required. Find the lowest-cost newspaper you can to do this. You do not have to publish with the big-city daily.

4. Submit the Articles of Organization form along with the fee. Make sure you pay any fees to the state on an annual basis. You want to make sure the state doesn't revoke your charter for failing to pay the fees.

Draw Up Your Documents: The documents you need for establishing a partnership include the offering circular, the operating agreement and the purchasers questionnaire. Let's look at each one individually.

Let's start with the offering circular. This is the document that clearly describes the deal specifics, including location and all the physical characteristics about the property. It should also include detailed information about the market in which the property is located and what the trends have been. In essence, the offering circular should cover everything an investor might want to know—the good and the bad—without fluff. It should also include projected, conservative pro formas of how you expect the property to perform. I say "conservative" here because you want to make sure you are not overselling or, in truth, selling at all. Your investment opportunity should be so financially sound it sells itself. Your attorney will review this document to ensure it is within the confines of the law. When it comes to real estate investments, even if your brother is your partner, the rules of law apply and the law says "salesy" solicitation is not allowed.

You will not have all the details of your potential investment at this stage, of course, but that should not stop you from compiling the boilerplate information—the stuff that will not change or that is not deal specific—and the market information. There's plenty you can prepare in advance from research you should already have done.

The second document you will need, and your attorney can help you draft it, is the actual operating agreement. This is the legal document that spells out the organizational matters, including the structure of the LLC; discloses all the partners; capital distributions; management; budgets and accounting elections; transfers and withdrawals; dissolution and termination; tax matters; and more. Again, you will not have the deal specifics at this point, but there's no reason to delay in getting the general agreement drafted. You can add the specifics of the deal once you know them.

You'll also need to have on file a purchaser's questionnaire. This questionnaire is designed to make sure that your investors are either "accredited," "sophisticated," or "high net worth." The U.S. government and every state has its own terminology, but the fact remains: only those "persons of means" as defined by each individual state and the Securities and Exchange Commission of the United States can invest in deals such as the ones you'll likely be doing. An attorney once told me if Uncle Bill wants to put $50,000 into your deal, walk away. But if Uncle Bill wants to put $500,000 into the deal, it may be worth taking on an unaccredited investor.

The reason you are looking for accredited investors is because the amount of legal filing and paperwork required to work with people who are unaccredited is cost prohibitive in most deals, particularly smaller ones. The red tape is exorbitant and the value minimal. As a rule, I only take on partners who are considered accredited.

Share Your Offering With Those You Trust: In most cases, you cannot directly advertise your offering. There are new rules for public "crowdfunding" efforts. More information is found in the book, *Finance You Own Business*. Overall, you must be careful with any offering of securities. This is federal law, and every state has its nuances about what constitutes solicitation and what does not. For complete information about what you can and cannot do, consult your attorney.

From there, you will have some who want to sit down and talk with you about the opportunity and others who will not be interested. Again, even verbally, I make sure when I have these sit-down meetings that I am not over selling or blue-skying the deal. I want people to know that these things are not sure things. That there is risk involved and that any partner I take on is willing to share in the risk as well as the reward. That's what a true partnership is, after all.

The money side of this business is not really as hard as it seems. There have been periods when it's been harder than others, when banks have tightened up lending and when other investments have seemed so hot, that people were putting their investment dollars there instead of in real estate. The Internet bubble comes to mind when everyone was pouring money into high-flying stocks. Of course, many of them crashed and burned, which means wealth on paper went up in smoke, too. People had less capital to move into real estate during those times.

The biggest example of this kind of hot and cold investment climate is what Peter Linneman, author of the quarterly real estate research newsletter *The Linneman Letter*, calls the Great Capital Strike of 2008. We're living with the aftermath of the government bank bail outs and credit freezes that have changed the rules. To show you in specific numbers how the Great Capital Strike affected real estate, here's a personal example. In 2006 before the crisis, we bought twenty-six acres of land and paid $5 million in cash. A year later, we took a $1.7 million loan out to improve the property and divide it into finished lots. After that, the property had appreciated to an appraised value of $8 million. When the loan came due in 2008, the lender required us to pay down the loan $500,000, bringing the loan to $1.2 million on a property worth $8 million. That translates into a 15-percent loan-to-value, which is the ratio between how much is owed and the property value. That might not mean much to you until you consider that *before* the Great Capital Strike, the loan-to-value would have been a minimum—*a minimum*—of 50 percent. In other words, it would have been perfectly acceptable to a lender to have a $4 million loan on a property valued at $8 million.

But what you'll find as you continue your path of real estate investor is that there are people out there who believe in real estate, and no matter what other "hot" investment is out there, they still want to put their stake in real estate. No matter what the lending requirements are, they work their deals the way they need to work them. The more people you meet, talk with, and build relationships with, the more people you will find who fit this description. As I said before, when the deal is right and the numbers work out favorably with enough cushion, you'll find the money you need. I'm confident of that.

PREPARING FOR WEEK 7

In the coming week, we're going to be taking that "maybe" pile of properties you've been looking at and narrow them down. At this point, you'll want to prepare yourself for some number crunching and review your HP calculator tutorial training. You'll also want to be sure your OMs are handy and that all the important numbers are on them or that you have got them in the file. Finally, you'll want to take out that formula cheat sheet and refresh your memory on the calculations important to determining the value of a property. This is the fun part because this is where you find the hidden gems!

CHAPTER 9

NARROW YOUR OPTIONS AND PICK THE WINNERS

WEEK 7 OF 9

It's Week 7 and by now you are deep into your own real estate life. You've met a number of new people in your community and you've been places, looking at buildings, thinking about money, and talking deal talk like a budding pro. Well, congratulations! You are on your way and things are heating up. How are the properties you're considering looking at this point? Do you have on your desk or in a binder a small "maybe" pile of ones that seem like viable candidates? Well, if you do, that's excellent. You're right on track because in this chapter, I'll show you my methods for narrowing that field and picking the winners.

In Chapter 6, we went over the offering memorandum or OM, and you learned my concept of flagging the pros and the cons of each property. You also learned about my Six Non-Negotiables for a property. That's a quick, qualitative way to eliminate properties that aren't worth any more of your time. The ones that are left—the ones that had important green flags and no, or very few, red flags—are tougher to rank. The properties you're considering should also have passed my Six Non-Negotiables Test. Where we go from here enters into a quantitative realm. Yes, it is time to get that HP calculator back out because it's time to take a look at how each of these properties is going to perform, at least in theory at this point.

For you math lovers, this will be the fun part. For you folks who aren't big numbers fans, you may be dreading it. You shouldn't, though. The principles aren't complicated and the formulas are quite easy. In fact, you are already aware of some of them from Chapter 6. Whatever you do, keep going, and don't worry. I was no math wiz in school and certainly didn't have CPA firms banging down my door offering me jobs after college. Good thing. If that had been me, I probably wouldn't have found such a great career and life in real estate.

In this chapter, we'll go over how to perform what's known as preliminary due diligence on a property so we can uncover the problems and opportunities (we're still looking for those flags). We'll cover how to quickly assess the financial performance of a property and compare it to the performance of other properties. And we'll go into detail on analyzing tenants, a very critical factor when evaluating commercial property. It's time to narrow your options to your top one or two properties.

PERFORMING VALUATION

Valuation, in my world, is the process of assembling the information I need to determine which properties are worth any more of my time. I start with a detailed look at the first property in my "maybe" pile and do a financial analysis on it. I do the same for all the others, and then compare the findings. You can do the same. This information all comes from the OMs and from the information you have gleaned from the professionals you have met with over the last few weeks. It also comes from comps and looking at alternative real estate investments. The prices other similar properties sold for is critical.

Real estate investing is all about information, so there's no time like the present to begin filling in the financial data on properties on your computer. I use a special tool—more on that later—to track all the important information. There are three methods that I use to value a building after I've narrowed down the choices:

Valuation Based on the Comps: Comps allow you to look at what range a property of this type should cost. I look at all properties that have been sold within the last six months, sometimes the last year. I look at the similar buildings, similar price range, similar size, with similar location to see how much they have sold for. The goal is to get a feel for where this property should be trading. I compare this to our building's asking price. I use a Comp Comparison Spreadsheet and record what I think the property I'm considering is worth and what it should sell for.

As I mentioned earlier, you can purchase comp information for the property you are considering. Information is also available online, but you'll have to do more research and compiling to arrive at meaningful comparisons. Purchased comps are assembled into reports, and by now you should have comps on each product you are considering. If you don't, take time now to pull a few comps for similar properties. Record the actual sales price, the building square footage, and the cost per square foot into the corresponding cells on the comp analysis spreadsheet. In the "comments" area of the spreadsheet, mark down any important details about the comparable buildings. Indicate the high and the low values.

Comp Comparison Spreadsheet

Subject Property	Property Address	Close of Escrow	Year Built	Square Feet	Sale Price	Price per Sq. Ft.	Cap Rate	Parking Ratio	Land Sq. Footage	Comments (pros, cons, etc.)
Comp 1										
Comp 2										
Comp 3										
Subject (Evaluation Price Range)	(This is the range we think the property should fall into based on evaluating the comps above.)									

Valuation Based on Replacement Cost: The second way to evaluate a property is to estimate how much it would cost to replace the building. The spreadsheet helps keep all the information organized. Here's how I do this analysis: The first thing I look at is the land. If this were a vacant lot, what would it trade for today? Land is a big part of the value of any property, and land costs can range anywhere from less than 10 percent of the overall property costs in high-rise buildings, for example, to as much as 35 percent of the property costs in buildings that are sitting on large parcels of land. Large warehouses are a good example, as are other buildings with large lot coverage. Many people don't think land value is important, but I do. Knowing the land value helps me establish a true value for the structure on that land. That's how I determine whether or not I am overpaying for a property. The other real benefit of this is, I can determine which properties I can buy at or below replacement costs.

To determine the replacement costs of the building, simply talk with your new-found contractors. People in the construction industry, including builders, architects, and other trades people, can give you an idea of what it would cost to build the same building today. It won't be exact, but it will be close enough for analysis purposes.

Following is an example of a replacement cost analysis I did recently for a property in Phoenix, Arizona, that I was considering:

BUDGET BREAK DOWN			
Location: 12345 Street Name Owner/Developer: Company Name, LLC			
Site & Building Improvements	**Total SF**	**$/SF**	**Total Building**
Base Building & Site (this pro forma includes 16,000 SF in mezzanine space)	64,000	$155.69	$9,964,313.76
BID BREAK DOWN			
PROJECT COSTS	**Base Building**	**$/SF**	**Total**
Land Cost ($15.00 per land sq. ft.)	**$2,723,220**	**$42.55**	
Building			
Off-Site	$350,000	$5.47	
Site Improvements	$0	$0.00	
Shell/Core	$2,790,984	$43.61	
Mezzanine Shell/Core	$448,000	$7.00	
Contingency	$0	$0.00	
Total Building	**$3,588,984**	**$56.08**	
Architectural & Engineering			
Due Diligence	$5,000	$0.08	
Civil Engineering	$27,000	$0.42	
Architecture Shell/Core	$120,000	$1.88	
Total A&E	**$152,000**	**$2.38**	
Miscellaneous Costs			
Permits/TAP/Impact Fees	$22,000	$0.34	
Marketing Costs	$7,500	$0.12	
Legal	$40,000	$0.63	
Construction Interest	$200,000	$3.13	
Financing Fees (bp)	$28,252	$0.44	
Misc. Financing	$10,000	$0.16	
Contingency	$160,245	$2.50	
Property Taxes	$5,000	$0.08	
Insurance	$13,000	$0.20	
Total Misc. Costs	**$485,997**	**$7.59**	
Development Fee	**$338,095**	**$5.28**	
Profit	**$2,112,000**	**$33.00**	
Subtotal	$9,400,296	$146.88	
Sales Commissions at 6%	$564,017.76	$8.81	
Total Cost	*$9,964,314*	*$155.69*	

If I can buy the building for less than the replacement cost, then I am interested. If I can't then I keep looking.

Valuation Based on Cash Flow Analysis and Net Operating Income: The third way to evaluate property is to determine, to the best of our abilities, how the investment will perform. In other words, we take a look at how much money we initially invest and then project to the end of the investment to see what kind of money we get back out of it. With the other two investment analysis methods, you have the help of consultants and advisors, but this third analysis is where things can get a little hairy. Here you must do your own assessments, and at this stage, you're just learning. It took me years to perfect my analysis methods and gain true confidence.

If we're going to look at the property you're considering as an investment, that will mean we will want to get out of that investment four important benefits:

- *Appreciation:* I want the property to grow in value.

- *Cash flow:* I want to derive a monthly dividend from my investment based on the property's operations.

- *Leverage:* I want to use other people's money to achieve appreciation and cash flow, not all my own.

- *Depreciation:* I want favorable tax treatment to minimize my annual taxes.

Understand, however, even though these four things are benefits of real estate, I want a real estate deal to work without taking appreciation or depreciation into account. The deal has to make sense without thinking about these things, which I consider icing on the cake. We also must understand that real estate is a risk, and we want to minimize risk. Here's how I keep things simple, so everyone—even those new to the business—can understand the principles, use them, and achieve a good outcome.

When I'm considering a property, cash flow is the thing I care about most. The method I use to project cash flow comes from the CCIM Institute. CCIM stands for Certified Commercial Investment Member, and the Institute is dedicated to education, networking, and the technology of real estate investing. The coursework is excellent, and by completing coursework, you can get your CCIM designation. In their financial analysis seminar, they review the concept of t-bars. A t-bar is the tool I use to help me map out the projected cash flow of a property and then compare it to the projected cash flow of other properties I may be considering. People call this a "napkin pro forma." It keeps things really simple and you get a picture of exactly what you are getting into with an investment. With just a few calculations, you can see if the deal you are looking at makes money sense and common sense. Let's drill down to more detail on this.

What's Included in the Initial Investment

Due Diligence Costs

    Demographic, market and/or traffic studies

    Geotechnical studies (or updates)

    Environmental reports (or updates)

    Building inspection costs—to determine potential capital expenses

    Legal expenses—title & survey review, agreement documentation

    Other professional fees

Financing Costs

    Loan fees

    Legal expenses

    Lender expenses

    Appraisal fee

    Insurance required by lender

    Title endorsements required by lender

    Civil engineer—survey updates required by lender

Building Costs

    Tenant improvement costs for non-leased space

    Commissions for non-leased space

    Any capital improvements that might be necessary

    Utility bonds or deposits for service

General Closing Costs

    Title and escrow fees

    Tax proration

    Sales commissions

FIRST, DEFINE THE TERMS

Initial Investment: Includes your initial down payment on the property plus all the costs to perform your due diligence work, your Phase 1 studies (which are part of your preliminary physical building inspection costs), closing costs, and any other out-of-pocket costs. Here's what I include in the initial investment number:

Determining and Validating a Property's Cash Flow

NET OPERATING INCOME =

<u>Gross Income</u>

Rent

Parking

% of Sales

Expense Reimbursements

Late Fees

Interest Income

<u>Less: Operating Expenses</u>

Repair & Maintenance

Janitorial

Landscaping

Security

Management

Utilities

Property Taxes

General & Administrative

CASH FLOW =

Net Operating Income

Less:

Debt service

Taxes (excluding property taxes)

Distributions

Leasing expenses (typically amortized for accounting purposes)

Capital expenses (typically amortized for accounting purposes)

NET PROFIT (for accounting purposes) =

Net Operating Income

Less:

Current portion of any amortized expenses

Interest expense

Depreciation

Taxes (excluding property taxes)

Cash Flow: This is how much money you project the property will yield after paying your loan, after capital improvements, after commissions, and after vacancies. Sometimes in the early years of an investment, cash flow is negative, which means that instead of money flowing out of the investment and into your pocket every month, money is flowing into the investment. In other words, you'll be paying in, and cash flow will be a cost. One of the biggest questions I get from people who are outside of the industry is how I go about validating the cash flow of a property. Like everything else, I have a system for it that has been honed over the course of my career. These are the numbers I seek at this point and the system for how they should all add up.

Sales Proceeds: This term refers to the money you gain from the sale of an investment and is defined as the net sales proceeds after you pay off expenses that include closing costs, commissions, prorations, the loan, etc. Here are the values I use to calculate this important number.

Calculating Sale Proceeds

PURCHASE PRICE

Plus:

    Non-refundable, non-applicable deposits

    Any tax credits

Less:

    Commissions

    Holdbacks (Tenant Improvements and/or Commissions)

    Legal expenses

    Title and escrow fees

    Loan pay-off

Other Adjustments:

    Rent and expense proration

= GROSS PROCEEDS

    Less:

        Reserve for post-close expenses

        Equity interest

        Equity return

    = NET PROCEEDS (PROFIT)

Understandably, these terms may still seem a little bit vague. Take the term "initial investment" for instance. At this stage, even though you know what goes into the initial investment, you may not have exact numbers and costs. Estimate them at first using your advisors and your own best judgment. The OM most likely has the numbers you need, so use it at this stage of the analysis. Then later during the due diligence period, when you collect all the facts, you can plug in the actual numbers and see if the investment still looks like one worth your time.

Cash flow can be a bit tricky, too. I always err on the side of being ultra conservative with my projections when it comes to cash flow. Here are some tips:

- If I project cash flow to be negative for the first two years, I put these amounts into my initial investment. That way I know what I will have to put into this property. As you can guess, this is a good practice, particularly if you have partners. By putting those early-year costs into the initial investment, I raise all the capital I need right up front. There is no calling investors for more money later.

- You may also be wondering how you actually know the values that go into the cash flow for a property. At this stage, as mentioned earlier, it comes from the OM. The key here is verifying each category to make sure their values are true and accurate. Early in the process, this means calling the owner and the tenants. Later, during due diligence it will mean reviewing tenants, leases, rents, and more. For now, using the numbers off the OM will tell you if the property is in the ballpark. Validating by phone the OM's accuracy is a good idea. This effort may even uncover some missed revenue opportunities that will bring additional cash flow.

WHAT A T-BAR LOOKS LIKE

T-bars are the CCIM Institute tools I use to logically depict how money flows into and out of a property over time. On the left-hand side of the table is a "time" column. Time can be years, months, quarters, whatever you want it to be. I typically use months and that's what is implied in this book. Time 0 is the day of close on a new property or that day when the cash was required to acquire the property. On the right-hand side is the "dollars" column and it shows the cash flow—either the dollars going out (in parentheses) or the dollars coming in (without parentheses). In essence, positive cash flow is shown without parentheses; negative cash flow is shown with parentheses.

Time	Dollars
0	(initial investment)
1	Cash flow
2	Cash flow
3	Cash flow
4	Cash flow
n	Cash flow + sale proceeds

(Used with permission CCIM Institute.)

Now let's look at a t-bar for a specific property. In this example, the initial investment was $4 million. At time period (months) 1 through 3, we projected a positive cash flow. During Month 4, this t-bar projected a negative cash flow of $32,420 because a tenant was vacating and we had some planned maintenance. At period *n* we predicted a positive proceed from the sale of the property. I created this t-bar using the values from a property's OM. Later, once the property has passed this initial test, and assuming it passes my other criteria, I'll do the work of validating the numbers. Why do the work of validating if the property doesn't make sense from the numbers on the OM?

PROPERTY 1

Time	Dollars
0	($4,000,000)
1 month	$76,775
2	$76,775
3	$76,775
4	($32,420)
|	|
Year 15	$9,500,000

As you can see, this property is still in the running. Cash flow is mostly positive and, at year *n*, I projected to have a significant positive return from that month's cash flow and sales proceeds. Looks pretty good, but the next step I take is to compare this property with two other alternative properties I considered to see which one looks the best. That's the only way we can determine the best investment choice.

No Short Cuts—Evaluate Alternative Property Investments

By developing t-bars for alternative investments, you are building the library of deals that you may want to chase. Later, you can look at the t-bars and see which deals were better than others. Once the buildings sell, I like to look at the comps of what they sold for and see how far off I was, or if I was right on. Further, I look at the comps in relationship to the current market to see if I was valuing according to the market. If it isn't obvious by now, this is all a process of getting intimate with every property you are interested in and the market as a whole. See why focus and narrowing your options is so important? There's no way you or anyone else could or would want to do this level of analysis for multiple asset classes.

Once you know how much money you project you'll have to put into an investment, and how much you think you'll get back, you can begin performing cash-on-cash calculations to see which property performs the best.

Cash on Cash: This calculation tells me how much money I am going to get on an annual basis, divided by how much money I put in. Recall this formula is simply:

Annual Income ÷ Annual Dollar Investment = Cash on Cash

So let's look at an example: This is a return <u>on</u> your money … not a return <u>of</u> your money.

Put in	Year	Return	Cash on Cash
$100,000	1	$6000	6%
	2	$12,000	12%
	3	$42,000	42% (sold property for $130,000)

In this example, we sell the property in Year 3 for $130,000, which is $30,000 more than my original $100,000 investment. That yields a $30,000 gain in addition to the $12,000 annual operating income, or $42,000 that year. That would equate to a 42-percent cash on cash return. Not bad!

I like the cash-on-cash calculation because it allows me to look at what kind of return I am getting on my money. It's a good way to see how well I'm doing with cash flow.

Internal Rate of Return: The internal rate of return (IRR) is an analysis tool used by more sophisticated investors. I look at it and use it as a more sophisticated tool when a property is in escrow, when I really want to know and understand the details of more complicated deals that have lots of tenants and longer-term holds. IRR allows you to analyze your investment with the subsequent cash flows, both positive and negative, and gives you a percent of return based on those values. The one drawback is that it assumes you reinvest the funds that you get out at the same IRR. The positive is that this calculation tells you what you got out of a series of transactions—for example, on those occasions when I put $100,000 into a property, got $1,000 out, put $10,000 in, took another $2,000 out, etc. This isn't something you can do on a napkin. It takes your HP calculator for sure. If you're a Microsoft Excel buff, it will calculate IRR automatically.

The times when I may use IRR calculations are when I'm trying to sell a property and want to find the property's best light and the way it is viewed the best by prospective buyers. Don't use it in your early evaluations to try to get the numbers to look good. If the numbers don't look good on a napkin and a simple T-square, move on. For me, it's all about how much money am I putting down, how much am I going to get back, and how much I get to keep. Some sophisticates may say this is Pollyana-ish, but to me it's not when we hit a recession and *they're* using fuzzy math to get their deal to work and *I'm* using real numbers.

ENOUGH INFORMATION TO DECIDE

Based on all this, we have what a typical building should cost. We also have what it would cost to replace this building today. We have a pretty good estimate of the initial investment, the projected cash flow, and even what a sale may bring us down the road. We have what the performance of the building looks like over time from the t-bar. Now we have the information to help us decide whether this is worth pursuing further. Recognize that pursuing this deal further will mean costs to you, so you want to be as sure as you can be at this point. The good news is that you've done this analysis on multiple properties, so you know which one looks the best compared to the others.

There are other areas you can look at and other ways to evaluate a deal. But these evaluations—based on the comps, based on replacement cost, and based on net operating income and cash flow—is enough to tell you whether you have a good deal or a bad deal. If you want to do more sophisticated analysis, there are ways to do it. One I recommend is to take a CCIM class. You don't have to do this to be a successful investor, particularly if you are buying smaller investments with ten or fewer tenants. Your gut is the most important thing. If all three of these indicators give you green lights, then it's a good deal. If one comes up red and the other two indicators are green, then you have to look at the specifics of the deal more closely or move on to other deals that are all green.

Speaking from experience, I like to know that someone can't come in and replicate what I'm buying at or near my cost. So for me, I either buy the building that is "special," meaning the location is irreplaceable, or buy the commodity building that is below replacement cost. I like to buy buildings that are 30 percent below replacement, so that my operating costs can be lower than the other guys'. That gives me the unfair advantage. I'm always ethically looking for the unfair advantage.

FINAL WORDS OF WISDOM

People get into trouble with real estate because they are buying properties with no cash flow or negative cash flow, banking on the appreciation. That's not my kind of investment because when the market declines—and you know it will because there is a real estate cycle—the property value declines. Or maybe the property owner loses a tenant, and the cash flow becomes even less than before. The debt is still out there and, if the property value declines significantly, not only may the owner be upside down on the loan—meaning owing more than the property is worth at the time—the owner may also be feeding that loan with less operating income than before. It can get ugly pretty quickly if you don't do your homework and base your deal decisions on cash flow, cash flow, cash flow. Go out and look for the investors that didn't heed this warning. Their properties are your buying opportunities!

PREPARING FOR WEEKS 8 AND 9

This is the big step, so get ready to make the call to say you are interested in the property. Of course there is more to it than that, and in the next chapter, you'll learn the right way to make an offer and negotiate the deal. This generally happens through the brokers, so there are no attorney fees to worry about yet. But get ready for that, too, because if your offer is accepted, the weeks to come will require the best help of your team—and as you can imagine, the best help costs money.

CHAPTER 10

MAKE AN OFFER AND NEGOTIATE THE DEAL

WEEKS 8 AND 9 OF 9

Congratulations! By now you have your target property. It's been quite a learning experience I'm sure. I learn something—many things—with every deal I do, even though I've been in the business for more than twenty years. That's what keeps it fresh and exciting.

In weeks 8 and 9, your learning will continue as we move into making and negotiating an offer. Now that you've found the property that meets your needs and your investment criteria, it's time to move the deal to the next phase. For many, this can be a bit scary at first, but don't let it be. This is about the numbers and the specifics of the deal, and in actuality, it can be and is pretty fun. Best of all, there is a standard process to negotiating the deal, so once you know it, you know it.

The process begins with a letter of intent, or LOI, also known as an offer document, that discusses the most important deal points. This is where the bulk of the negotiation actually happens. We'll go over the most important deal points and show some examples. It's important to have a feel for what is ordinary, what is extraordinary, and what the typical give-and-takes are for a deal, although every deal is different. Our goal—your goal—is to make these documents as favorable to you as possible.

WHAT'S A LETTER OF INTENT?

According to InvestorWords.com, an excellent resource for you and anyone who wants to know what an investment term means, a letter of intent is defined as follows:

> *"A letter from one company to another acknowledging a willingness and ability to do business… A letter of intent is not a contract and cannot be enforced, it is just a document stating serious intent to carry out certain business activities."*

Interesting. Why should so much effort be put into a document that isn't legally enforceable? There's good reason. The goal of the letter of intent is to hash out all the details of a deal before the deal gets to the contract stage and attorneys get involved. Contract negotiations can get expensive. A letter of intent enables two parties to negotiate and confirm all the key points in advance of drafting the contract. The ultimate goal is to have the contract phase breeze through without much revision. If the letter of intent process is managed properly, achieving that goal is possible.

In commercial real estate, there is no standard contract. Well, actually, there is, but no one uses it. An attorney is always required. The letter of intent gets the main deal points on the table before you're on the clock with an attorney. I've saved thousands of dollars in attorney fees for deals that weren't really deals—the ones that were going forward until the deal points were laid out. Then for one reason or another, it was no deal. That cost me nothing but my time which is valuable enough.

MANAGING THE PROCESS

Letters of intent are generally drafted by the buyer, and managing the letter of intent process well is one of the things that separate the weak investors from the strong. The good news is that your broker will help you, but I advise knowing what effective letter of intent management is all about. Specifically, it involves knowing what key points the letter will cover. It means knowing your desired outcomes for each point. It means knowing the timeframe and pushing a timeline. It also means solidly communicating throughout the process with your broker.

Every commercial letter of intent should include the following key points:

- Basic property information
- Inspection/feasibility period
- Escrow and title work
- Property condition
- Prorations and closing costs
- Possession
- Close of escrow
- Commission
- Expiration Date

Let's discuss each one in a bit more detail.

Basic Property Information: This includes the property name, location, buyer, seller, purchase price (offer price), terms, due diligence period, free-look period length, representations and warranties of the buyer and seller, any hazardous materials declarations, etc. Obviously at this point, I make sure all this information is accurate. If or when the deal goes to contract, this information will be transferred into a binding legal agreement.

Inspection/Feasibility Period: This is a critical negotiation point because, in essence, this point will tell you how long you will have to perform your due diligence on the property. Remember, up to now, you were basing your evaluation on the OM, your gut, and your advisors' opinions. Typically, the inspection/feasibility time frame is sixty days, and even though this may seem adequate, there is much to do in a very short time. The last thing you want to be is rushed, and miss identifying a big problem with a property. That's how the devastating real estate investment mistakes happen.

During the due diligence process—even after the letter of intent is signed—you can terminate the deal should you find a problem with the property or the numbers. Negotiate for the most time you can get; this is not the time for shortcuts.

Escrow and Title Work: In this section of the letter of intent, you and the seller will define who will actually do the escrow and title work for the deal, the date when escrow will be opened, what the earnest money amount will be, whether it earns interest or not, and to who's benefit, and whether or not the earnest money is refundable should the deal fall apart during the inspection/feasibility period. Of course you want the earnest money to be refundable!

Property Condition: This section warrants that the seller will keep the property in current condition during the negotiation and closing period. It puts in writing that the seller does not know of any defects or hazards that he or she has not already disclosed to the buyer and it says the final purchase agreement will contain a paragraph to this effect. This is protection for the buyer and warns the seller that he or she better disclose any and all problems or face possible legal action in the future.

Prorations and Closing Costs: This section outlines who pays such things as closing costs, escrow fees, premiums for title insurance, and how property taxes will be prorated. Typically, the seller pays half of the escrow fee and the premium for a standard policy of title insurance. Property taxes are prorated as of the date the deed is recorded and you officially take over the property.

Possession: This section simply states when the buyer will take ownership of the property. It is generally upon the close of escrow.

Close of Escrow: The big day. This is when you sign all the papers to transfer ownership. Be sure to get all documentation in advance so you can review, make sure they are correct and ask any questions.

Commission: Here, the letter spells out the terms of the commission rate and who pays for it, the buyer or the seller. Generally commission is paid by the seller.

Expiration Date: Letters of intent also generally have an expiration date. This ensures that the deal keeps moving. Typically, I push for a ten-day window within which the seller has the opportunity to counter any of the key points, or sign the letter.

Below is an actual letter of intent for one of my deals that is fair but buyer-focused.

Sample Letter of Intent

April 21, 2013
Mr. John Doe
Company Name, LLC
1234 E. Main Street
Mytown, MyState 10000

RE: OFFER TO PURCHASE
3456 N. CENTER STREET, MYTOWN, MYSTATE

Dear John:

Brokerage Company, on behalf of Company Name, LLC and/or assignee, would like to present this offer to purchase the 3456 N. Center Street building subject to the following terms and conditions. This offer is not a binding contract between Buyer and Seller for the purchase and sale of the Property and neither party shall be so legally bound until such time as and unless all the details are agreed and the Purchase and Sale Agreement and related documentation have been executed and exchanged.

Property: 3456 N. Center Street, a 40,021 square foot building

Buyer: Company Name, LLC and/or assignee

Purchase Price: $4,500,000.00

Terms: Cash at close of escrow

Inspection/
Feasibility Period: Buyer shall have sixty (60) days from Opening of Escrow (the "Inspection/Feasibility Period") to conduct all studies, tests, reviews and other due diligence. Final approval to move forward beyond the feasibility period shall be in the buyer's sole discretion, without limitations. Buyer shall be entitled to enter and inspect the property a reasonable number of times after acceptance of this letter. The following items are to be provided by Seller:

1. Current ALTA Survey

2. Any as-builts or construction drawings for the building

3. Four years property tax bills and complete operating expense information, including 2005 YTD operating expenses and actual operating expenses for the previous four (4) years.

4. Any documents in Sellers possession regarding Special Improvement Districts, CC&R's and assessments that Seller may have in its possession, without obligation for producing documents not readily available to Seller.

- Phase I Environmental Report

- All existing leases

- List of all pending and historical legal actions regarding the property to the extent Seller has actual knowledge of such action

- Any contracts Seller has entered into

Seller agrees to provide Buyer a Preliminary Title Report and the aforementioned documents within five (5) days after the Opening of Escrow, Buyer shall have fifty-five (55) days after receipt of the Preliminary Title Report and current ALTA Survey to review and approve in writing. Failure by Buyer to provide written approval of the Preliminary Title Report and current ALTA Survey within such fifty-five (55) days shall be deemed to be Buyer's disapproval.

Escrow and Title Work: The Escrow shall be deemed to be opened upon the Escrow Agent's (Name Title Agency) receipt of the fully executed Purchase Agreement (which shall include Escrow Instructions) and a fifty thousand and no/100 dollars ($50,000.00) Earnest Money Deposit. The Deposit shall earn interest, which shall accrue to the benefit of the Buyer and shall apply toward the purchase price. The deposit shall be fully refundable during the Inspection/Feasibility period. If Buyer elects to cancel during the Inspection/Feasibility period, at Buyer's sole discretion, then the deposit shall be refunded immediately.

Prorations and Closing Costs: At Closing, Seller shall pay one-half (1/2) of the escrow fee, the premium for a standard policy of title insurance for the amount of the Purchase Price and other costs properly chargeable in accordance with the prevailing custom in Phoenix, Arizona. Property taxes shall be prorated as of the date of recordation of the Deed. Special assessments, if any, are to be paid by Seller.

Property Condition: Seller will warrant to maintain Property in its current condition during the Escrow. Seller warrants that it possesses no actual knowledge of any hazards and that it has not received any notice from any government agencies regarding violations of, including but not limited to, Zoning, Building, Environmental, or Eminent Domain.

The Final Purchase and Sale Agreement shall contain such other standard representations and warranties as are mutually acceptable to Buyer's and Seller's counsel.

Possession: Possession shall be delivered to Buyer upon Close of Escrow.

Close of Escrow: The Close of Escrow shall be not later than thirty (30) days after the end of the "Inspection/Feasibility Period."

Commission: Buyer and Seller acknowledge that a commission equal to fifty percent (50%) of the total brokerage fee shall be due to Lee & Associates Arizona at Close of Escrow, to be paid by Seller.

If the foregoing is acceptable, please sign below and return a copy of this offer to my attention. This offer will expire within ten (10) days of receipt.

Please feel free to call me if you have any questions.

Best Regards,

Brokerage Company
Craig Coppola, CCIM, CRE, SIOR
Principal

Approved and accepted this _____ day of _____, 20XX

SELLER

By: _____

Its: _____

Approved and accepted this _____ day of _____, 20XX

BUYER

By: _____

Its: _____

THE FINER POINTS ABOUT LETTERS OF INTENT

This letter of intent is what you are shooting for. It didn't start out this way. The deal points within it took some time to negotiate. The letter of intent is designed to save you a ton of time and to enable you to put one or a bunch of offers out there for properties that fit the bill. It is the document that gives you the entrée to play the negotiation game. You may not get any of the deals, but it is an opportunity to have a dialogue with a seller.

Performing these steps well puts you in a very credible negotiation position. You can justify through the numbers how and why you are making the offer. You gain confidence knowing you're making the right offer, and, if it's accepted, you feel good about that, too.

As I said, not every offer gets accepted. Be prepared to get no reply, a "hell, no" reply, or a counter offer at the offering price. When that happens, you can give the seller a summary of the numbers you used to arrive at the offer price, but you have to be prepared to walk away. I lose more properties than I win, and if I win more than I lose, I know I'm overpaying.

This dance of give-and-take involves time. It's time well spent, particularly when you work to secure the most important deal points in your favor. To me, those are the due diligence period and the earnest money. The money is usually refundable for a period of time—usually thirty to sixty days—but still, this is an important negotiation point. You will need those funds for other expenses—expected or unexpected—during the due diligence process. Plus, low earnest money amounts may allow you to work several deals at once. There's a saying, "If I give you your price, you give me my terms. If I give you your terms, you give me my price." Think of it that way, then have your own solid strategy for each opportunity.

DEVELOPING YOUR NEGOTIATION STRATEGY

My negotiation strategy is simply to position the offer at a reasonable price, but clearly not where I am going to end up. I show the seller that I have done my homework, so he or she knows that I know what I'm doing. I don't just throw offers out there. I always make sure they are in the ballpark. Then I use the letter of intent to get all the deal points out on the table before an attorney is involved. If you need financing, put it in the LOI. If you're worried about due diligence, put it in the LOI.

I test the waters by calling the broker first and saying, "Here's what I think the building is worth. Is it worth my time to put an offer in?" If the broker says, "Yes" or "The owner is eager to sell," then I have more information than if I put the offer in blindly. It's all about showing you have done your research. The LOI isn't just putting it together; it's about closing the deal.

Deal breakers primarily come in three flavors. Price is first. You like the building, but you can't come to a price. Terms are the next flavor. The seller wants you to close really fast and you simply can't. The third issue is inaccurate information. The owner tells you the property has a certain cash flow, and then when you get into the property, you find out that it was overstated.

For me, each and every one of these are deal breakers because they often jeopardize the economics of the deal. Sure, I'll go back to my numbers and see if they still work, with adequate cushion, but generally they don't. And I'm certainly not going to rush through the due diligence phase—particularly after my first deal's $15,000 lesson—and potentially miss a big problem that will cost me a lot of money. No property is worth that risk. There are always others out there.

WHAT IF YOU'RE COMPETING?

In some cases, you may be the only investor interested in a particular building at a particular moment, but in other cases, a seller is fielding multiple offers. To that I say that all's fair in love, war, and real estate negotiation. There was one deal in which I had put in a lot of time. We finally got down to the letter of intent and I had faxed my offer to the seller's agent. Little did I know that another investor who wanted the same building was standing right by the fax machine. He saw my offer and knew if he offered $50,000 more he'd still have a good deal. You guessed it: he handed the broker the offer and said he'd offer an extra $50K, right on the spot. I lost the deal. Beyond the lesson of "anything can happen" is the lesson of preparedness. This guy, who had done his homework, was in the right place at the right time and was prepared to capitalize on an opportunity. You win some and you lose some, but assume a winner's attitude and a winner's zeal.

GET OUT THERE

Now that you know how offers and negotiations work, go out there and make some offers. Remember, you don't have to buy anything. Think of this as practice. Draw up your letters of intent. Call the selling broker and feel what it is like to work through this phase of the deal. It will take all the fear and the mystery right out of it, I promise you that. You never know, one deal may actually look like a winner. In that case, then it will be time to come to a decision. Are you ready to own your first commercial property investment or not?

PREPARING FOR THE POST-9-WEEKS PHASE

If you are to this point and you have submitted one or more offers, congratulations! You have really succeeded in your push to become a real estate investor. For as much hard work as you just accomplished, however, there is still more to go, particularly if none of your offers were accepted. As I mentioned, it happens a lot. That means your next weeks will be spent going back to the drawing board and finding more deals to analyze, compare, and offer for purchase. If one of the offers you submitted was accepted and you believe you want to move forward, then read on quickly because the clock of due diligence is ticking and there's much work to be done!

CHAPTER 11

DETAILED DUE DILIGENCE AND CLOSING

POST-9-WEEKS PHASE

In the last chapter, we reviewed the letter of intent and talked about the inspection/feasibility period. Well, allow me to state for the record that these sixty days may just possibly be the most important sixty days of your life as a real estate investor. This is the period when you perform your due diligence on the property, and within this time frame, your mission—and I know you will accept it—is to find out every problem and every opportunity with the property.

I love this part of the business because now I have a real deal in my grasp. I'm past all the speculation and I'm sixty to ninety days away from owning a property. With your investors' and/or your own weight on your shoulders, you have to make sure this is a good deal. This is the time when you're really delving into the property; you're past the first date and seeing all the pros and the cons, the opportunities and weaknesses. Everything you dig up about this property will help you in some way. It will either make you money, save you money, or give you reason to walk away. It will also give you the background data you'll need when you are ready to sell the property.

The remainder of this chapter will outline everything that you and your team will review during the due diligence process. It is a lengthy list, but this is where the team that you assembled earlier in the process really comes into its own. They are the ones who will perform much of the work, report back to you, and serve as your expert advisors. They are invaluable to this process. Your job, again, is project manager and the clock is ticking. Unlike a letter of intent where, if a deadline is missed, the document becomes void without legal or monetary ramifications, here, if the clock runs out and you have not completed your analysis, or backed out of the deal, you own the property, like it or not. Not a great position to be in. Manage your time wisely.

Finally, after due diligence work is done and you're moving full steam ahead, we'll cover the close of the deal. Yes, there will be champagne for everyone. Let's not get ahead of ourselves. There's work to do, starting with the property review.

Property Review

The property review is your opportunity to dig deeply into the specifics of the property itself. Much of the work here is hiring and scheduling your team of pros to do the work and advise you of their findings. Your other role, and it's a big one, is decision maker. What problems can you live with, what problems can be fixed without affecting your return on investment, and when do the shortcomings signal it's time to pull the plug on the deal? Those are important questions and your team can help you find the answers. Here's what is involved in a property review:

Order Physical Inspection and Get Due Date: People who do property inspections know how to find out what is wrong with the property, what needs to be updated, and what needs to be improved. Phase 1 inspectors do physical reviews and look for things like broken windows, clogged sinks, etc. You want to perform this work because, as the saying goes, caveat emptor (buyer beware).

The reality for me is that I always want to know what I'm buying, so as soon as that letter of intent is signed and I've decided to move to this phase, the first call I make is to my property inspector.

At this stage, I'm looking for big problems, like a $10,000 problem in a $100,000 property. That's a big problem. The key is to make sure the deal you have in hand is a good one. Problems of a grand scale will negatively impact your pro forma. Now, sometimes you can get the seller to pay to fix the problem—particularly if the seller is very motivated—but don't be surprised if the seller says, "No." By law, once a building defect is out in the open, the problem must be disclosed to other buyers, but there's nothing stopping the seller from minimizing the problem through a lax second opinion. My rule of thumb is that if a repair costs a significant amount of money, it will cost your bottom line a significant amount of money, too.

Zoning and Parking Verification: Understanding the zoning, use, and parking particulars of a building comprise the next critical review. For example, sometimes properties will be improperly zoned or are lacking permits for the tenant improvements (TIs) that have happened inside the building. Tenants often add unapproved, even illegal, improvements. This can cause fines, and, should you buy the building, you may be required to bring the premises to its former state, up to code, or both. I've heard of one instance where there was a bidding war on a property. The people who won the bid knew, as did the other bidders, that there were improvements in the property that were not up to code. After the deal was inked, a losing bidder turned the winners in and now the new owners are faced with the costs of bringing the building up to code.

Parking is another issue. Some buildings have too few parking spaces and don't meet the code for your city or state (typical now is five spaces per thousand square feet of building interior). What happens if you buy a building that is under parked with no room for additional spaces? It can absolutely mean trouble and be irreparable.

Another example of functional obsolescence relates to buildings that are not wheelchair accessible, or that don't comply with other Americans with Disabilities Act (ADA) requirements. Those can mean big costs, too. It's not that you disregard buildings that need work, but understand how to recognize a building where bringing it up to standard is feasible from one where bringing it to date is not. When bringing it up to date is feasible, how will the added costs affect your pro forma?

All Required Permits on File: Sometimes, buildings lack proper permits, as we described above, or the inspections happened but there was no follow-up on receiving the permits. This happened to me on one building. I had to pay to have the city re-inspect the building and issue the permit. I defer to my architect for assistance with this.

Certificate of Occupancy (Shell): If you're buying a new building, you'll need to have the shell inspected. Once it passes the inspection, you'll receive a Certificate of Occupancy which allows you to begin your TIs. Your architect or contractor will help you with this.

Certificate of Occupancy (TI): This certificate is for the TIs. At this point, it's important to review the CC&Rs (codes, covenants and restrictions), which are the rules and regulations for the building, dictated by the association controlling the project. These include such things as signage requirements/restrictions, hours, lights, trash pick up, extermination, public area maintenance, etc. This is my responsibility and the responsibility of the person who helps me with my research.

Review Association Documents: Some buildings are part of an association and have certain requirements and restrictions. This is part of the CC&R review. I look at all the documents and see what the restrictions are. Are those restrictions going to inhibit my ability to lease the building? I trust my property management team to help me with this.

Review the Close-out Manual: I always look at what is called the close-out manual for new buildings. These include all the warranties and owner's manuals for everything from air conditioners to toilets and everything in-between.

FINANCIAL REVIEW

Just as there is a property review, there is a financial review. It covers all the information required by the lender to help you secure your financing. Here are the particulars of what the lender is looking for.

Prepare Finance Package, Get Terms, Prepare Matrix for Evaluation, Select Lender: At this stage, my team and I prepare a finance package that overviews the property. You can do this yourself or have a finance person help you. Lenders want to know what they are financing and specifically are looking for things like cash flow of the tenants, expenses, lease summaries, project overview, and set of plans. In essence, you're painting a picture of the property and why the lender should invest in it. We have one pro forma that goes to the lender that is accurate and shows the solid potential. The goal here is to draw up the documents so that you get the most money you can from the lender. Here's the checklist I use:

Project Name & Location ACQUISITION DUE DILIGENCE	
	Item Required (General Description)
FINANCIAL REVIEW	
	Operating Statements—3 fiscal years
	Property Management Reports—last 12 months
	List of all capital expenditures in the last 5 years
	Leases and Lease Abstracts
	Tenant Financials (as required)
	Recent Appraisal (if available)
APPRAISAL PACKAGE (All of the above, plus)	
	Site Plan and Floor Plans
	Building Plans & Specs
	Site Survey (ALTA)
	Title Report (w/Schedule B back-up)
	Environmental Report (Phase I, other as available or required)
	Visuals—Photos, Aerials, etc...
	General Construction Information
	Property Tax Information (APNs)—including any special assessments
LENDER ITEMS (All of the above, plus)	
	Copies of all Vendor Contracts & Service Agreements
	Utility Statements for the last 12-Months
	Any Building Warranties
	Close-out Binder

Prepare Partner Finance Package, Get Commitments: This is an accurate and realistic pro forma for the property, but it is framed in a way that is not as optimistic as the one prepared for the lender. The goal here is to be pragmatic and set up realistic expectations for the investor. This document should clearly communicate the pros and cons as well as the risks. A good partner is a realistic, informed partner. They call less often!

Forward Due Diligence Package to Lender ASAP (Four-Week Lead Time): After you select the lender, he or she will want to do an appraisal. Knowing that the clock is ticking and appraisal lead times can be as long as four weeks or more, you want to move on this very quickly. Remember, you only have so much time to complete the whole due diligence process, and the last thing you want is to be held up because of an appraisal. Miss the due diligence deadline and you could lose the deal. This is why it's important to have relationships with key people. I have relationships with the appraisers. When I'm in a pinch, I can call on a handful of people I can count on for fast response.

Lender Estoppels/SNDAs (Two- to Three-Week Lead Time): When a building owner prepares to sell a building, the owner must get a signed estoppel form from every tenant that verifies the lease amount, its terms, and its duration. Most of the time, the landlord does the estoppels and then you verify them with the tenants themselves. It's an extra step worth doing.

INCOME REVIEW

The following reviews relate to the income generating potential of the property.

Review and Abstract Leases: At this stage, you take a look at all tenant leases and summarize them. Term, name of tenant, who the signatory is, options to renew, options to grow, rent increases, etc.

Review Tenant Financials: Lenders and partners will want to know the financial condition of the tenants. This is very important. Businesses do fail, so minimize your risk by doing your homework for yourself as well as your lender. You have every right to meet with the tenants to discuss their economic outlook and then verify through annual corporation reports, tax filings, etc.

Tenant Satisfaction (Likelihood of Renewal): Understanding tenant satisfaction is not only a good way to determine the likelihood of renewal, it is where I learn everything about the building. This happens through personal interviews with tenants. Smart owners want to sit in on the meetings with you, because they know tenants will talk. Regardless, the questions I ask include the following: Tell me about your business. What are your likes and dislikes about this building? Is there anything wrong with the building? What would you change?

Recognize that sometimes you may buy a building because it is over-managed, not under-managed. The opportunity lies with taking things away and *saving* your way to increased cash flow. For example, one building I know of changed out the flowers in the planters and beds every month instead of once per season. The good news with buildings like this is that you are buying something that is well cared for, but some cost cutting measures that are meaningless to the tenants and the overall appearance can mean profits in your pocket.

Review Security Deposits/LOCs (Letters of Credit): It's always good to know each tenant's security deposit amount because if it is too low, you have very little coverage against damages. In my opinion, one month or two is low and doesn't afford you much protection in the event a tenant walks away from a lease.

Also check to see if any tenants have LOCs (letters of credit). These are lines of credit owners require tenants to get from the bank. The LOC functions as a guarantee that the bank will pay the owner the full lease amount or pay up to a predetermined level should the tenant default. Tenants can secure these for a few hundred dollars per year and in some cases use them to as a cash flow management tool. But they do afford some protection for the property owner.

Check Receivables for Collection History: Wouldn't you love to know which tenants are slow payers and which ones are behind in their rent payments? Of course you would. This information is critical to understanding the cash flow of the building and the health of the tenants. Take a look at the receivables history and you'll get your answer.

Check for Any "Other" Income: Other income can come from things such as parking fees for shaded covered parking and money made through vending machines. CAM (common area maintenance) fees provide another profit center, as does property management fees you pay yourself if your property is self-managed. These all need to be added into the mix. Lack of "other" income in an existing building may signal some terrific money-making opportunities.

Check Expense Reimbursements: Expense reimbursements are considered income. Sometimes expenses will be estimated—things like landscaping, maintenance, etc.—and will actually be less or more than expected. If the expenses are less than anticipated, the property management must reimburse tenants; if they are higher than estimated, then the tenants must pay additional dollars. Sometimes no expenses are levied to tenants at all, and these are opportunities to generate more cash flow. These are the kinds of things to look for during the due diligence phase—things that will cost you money and, better yet, opportunities people missed that can make you money.

EXPENSE REVIEW

Now that you know how the money flows into the property, it's time to look at how the money flows out—the expense side of the balance sheet.

Review Last Three Years' Tax Statements: Tax statements help you confirm full assessment value of the property or determine full assessment, whichever the case may be. At this point, I check for any special assessments that might apply as well as improvement districts, which can add a substantial amount to price of the land or property. By now you know how the building generates cash and have a very good idea of how much that is on an annual basis. When you buy a building, you cannot assume that the tax assessment of the building will match your own assessment. Sometimes assessments are outdated and the actual building operations perform better or worse than the current assessment. If the building is operating better than it was last year, the assessment is going to be higher and you'll want to plan for that in your tax strategy. Even more dramatic, if you bought property last year and it was raw land and this year there is a building on it, the property is going to assess higher. You get the idea.

Review Utilities—Gross Up Assumptions: At this point, I look at the utilities to get a projection of future expenses. Common sense says if I'm looking at a building that is 50-percent leased and the utilities are $3,000 per month, I can guess that when the building is 100-percent leased, the utility expenses are going to at least double. I look at variable expenses like electricity, janitorial, etc.

Confirm Reasonableness of Other Expense Items: Here, I look at management fees, administration costs, insurance, landscaping costs, and all the other costs in running the building. I determine whether they are too high and in some cases review in-depth management reports and operation statements to get a better understanding of the numbers. There are often ways to reduce costs, which again adds to the bottom line.

Review Annual Budget and Develop Your Own: At last, you can take a look at the big picture. The goal here is to get at the net operating income (NOI) figure, which, if you recall, equals income minus expenses. This is where you look at how the property is managed. What are the expenses? What is the current owner doing that you wouldn't do? What isn't the current owner doing that you would do and enable you to raise rents? Where can you save money? Where must you spend it? This is the time to develop your own budget for the property.

LEGAL REVIEW

By this stage, the investment is looking good on paper from a property standpoint and from a cash flow standpoint. There are some income and expense opportunities and you've put together a realistic budget that delivers a solid net operating income (NOI). Now it's time to review the legal aspects of the property. And allow me to emphasize this point: Be sure your attorney isn't a deal killer!

Title Review, Including Schedule B: This is when your attorney reviews the particulars of a property like easement issues, property lines, etc. They are listed in what are known as a schedule B. You want to know if there are any lien holders, any and all special assessments, covenants conditions and restrictions that limit the property's uses. For example, if the property you are considering has a utility easement like gas pipes or electrical underground, you can't build over the utility line. There may be paint color limitations, signage limitations, usage limitations, even lien holders who have claim to the building before you.

Survey Review—ALTA Survey: An ALTA (from the American Land Title Association) survey is a survey of the property that, along with the title report, gives you a good feel for the physical nature of the building and the restrictions placed on that building. For example, on an ALTA survey, all utilities are listed above and below ground. There may be underground gas lines or sewer lines that you cannot move and you cannot build on top of. There are hundreds of things that can affect a property and you'll be surprised at what you might find in an ALTA survey.

Soils Reports: Not all soil is created equal, and there are some substrates that make for great building foundations and some that do not. For most of the country, the soils report is part of the Phase 1 study. What you are looking for is if there is anything toxic on the property. Other issues can include compaction and whether or not the ground is suitable to house a building. With cracks in the foundation, sink holes can result.

Environmental Reports: Phase 1 is basic level. If they find anything during the initial inspection, they go to Phase 2, then 3. Are there any environmental issues, asbestos, water table and water issues, flood plain issues, easements, core samples? This can run you a few thousand dollars and up.

Partnership Document Preparation: Your attorney will review the loan documents. The attorney will prepare the LLC partner documents and these can be the basis for future deals. This is money out of pocket.

Purchase and Sale Agreement (PSA) Document Review: You might prepare this, or sometimes the seller prepares it. An attorney must create and/or review the purchase and sale agreement. This is the actual document that contains the terms to purchase the property. There is no standard document in the commercial real estate world, although it will state what you are buying and what the seller is going to give you in terms of representations and warranties—which oftentimes is none. A seller's minimum warranty is that I own the property and that I can sell it to you, as is, where it is. This is part of your negotiation process. To really drive home the importance of doing your homework, understand that most agreements have no warranties included. Should you find an inherent flaw with the building after you have signed the agreement, you are on your own. Some PSAs are detailed and some aren't.

Any Special Issues (CC&Rs, Associations, Zoning, or Variance):
All properties that are in municipalities have zoning classifications.
That zoning classification will tell you what you can and can't do
on the property. For example, if you have a property that is zoned
office and try to construct an industrial building, you won't be
successful. At least not without a rezoning of the property.
Properties may also have special use permits, special associations
that may further restrict what you can do. They may have
covenants, conditions and restrictions, more commonly known as
CC&Rs. These zoning issues and restrictions affect the value of
your property negatively or positively. Sometimes the limitations
are very favorable. If you own a property near a park, the value of
the property can be higher because people know there can never
be a tire recycling facility built next door.

FINANCIAL ASPECTS

With the legal review completed, it's time to take care of the financial
aspects of the impending close of the sale. This includes coordinating
all the documents (purchase, loan, and partnership) obtaining
required signatures, and, in essence, getting the paperwork together.
The buyer, the lender, and the title company work on this aspect of the
transaction. The bank takes care of all the loan documents; the title
company takes care of the acquisition documents; and you take care
of overseeing all of it. Plus, it's up to you to take care of your investors
and run down any other documents the lender and the title
company require.

Arrange Deposit Funding: You're going to put a deposit down, your
earnest money, so now's the time to have it ready to go.

Arrange Equity Funding: This is your partner funding—you, your
partners, and your lenders. It's one thing for them to say that
they'll give you money. It's another thing to get it from them. I've
found that on the really good deals, there isn't an issue with
getting the money. It's important to know who your really good
investors are. On one deal I knew about, the managing partner
had lined up people as investors who, literally, took him for a ride.

They were going to buy a jet hangar, but after numerous rides in jet-setter G4 aircraft, they never put the money up. A lot of expense all on a sham that was a massive loss of time and reputation.

Arrange Lender Funding: This is finalizing the financing with the lender. By this time, you have already talked with and, I hope, become very cozy with your lender. You should already be pre-approved for financing and know what your debt-to-equity ratio must be for any property you are looking to buy. Finally, it's time to fully review the settlement statement, which is the document that contains things like prorations, the price, the commissions, and the fees. This is the document that tells you where all the money is going, and it is your job to review the document to make sure the title company is allocating all of the funds properly.

Coordinate the Transfer of Asset: If you were ever wondering when the whole deal would start to feel real to you, you'll be pleased to know you're getting close at this point. This is the document that will plan out in full detail the transfer of the asset. Translated, that means your agent and the seller's agent and the seller will outline exactly when you will get the keys to the building, when all contracts will be assigned to you, when the former owner's tenants will become your tenants, when rent payments will have you as the payee instead of the former owner, and when the building accounting will be fully transferred to you. In addition, this document will define when expenses and services like utilities, maintenance, etc. will be your responsibility.

Financial Aspects Post Close: When you become a commercial real estate investor, particularly if you are the managing partner in a limited partnership and certainly if you are the sole owner, you have actually bought more than just a building. You have, in essence, bought a business that must be managed long term. That's a good thing, because, as I said in the first chapter, you get to be in control of your investments. For me, I like knowing that if I manage a building properly or hire a management company to do the work and manage the building properly, my asset can appreciate and throw off cash every month. Much of that comes down to managing the financial aspects of your investment. That means organizing documents and setting up your systems. It's a little extra work, but you'll thank me later.

Contact List Set-Up: An important step in taking care of your property investment well is being sure right from the get go that you have an accurate and complete list with the full information on tenants, vendors, and suppliers, along with anyone else involved in the property. I like to add to that list my partners and investors, too. All this goes into the property file or binder as well as in a property area on the computer so that communication and management is a breeze.

Copy of Appraisal: Here's another document you will want in the property file or binder and in an electronic version on your computer, and for just reason: When you sell the building, this is one of the many documents that the buyer will want to see. You simply acquire this document from the lender after the closing.

Copy of the Closing Binder: The title company or the lender puts this together for every deal and you are entitled to a copy for your own property file or binder. In this binder are all the documents that you signed for the building. I actually have binders for every property I own, and these documents comprise a large section of each one.

Prepare Calendar with Reporting Obligations: Yes, you are running a business when you buy commercial property whether you have partners or not, so developing systems to streamline your tasks will free up a lot of your time and make you more efficient. It took me a few properties to figure this out, but ever since then I make sure to develop the annual calendar for events and communication after I close on a property. You have to be organized, and you'll want to be organized. If you have partners, a calendar is a given because your investors will expect regular communications. If the property is cruising along and there are no big issues, communicating with your partners once per year may be fine. If you are new and your investors are new, once a quarter may be more realistic. There are other audiences you'll need to communicate with on a regular basis, like your tenants, your lender, and even your management company or any internal staff you eventually may hire.

Set Up Management Reports: Again, the better your systems, the more efficient you'll be. When I buy a property, I immediately set up my own reports for operations. They show budget variances by month, monthly income, monthly expenses, how monies are being spent and how monies are coming in. Following is the budget report I use, showing six months of projections:

Account Name	Jan	Feb	Mar	Apr	May	Jun
INCOME						
RENT INCOME						
Rent	$73,711	$73,711	$73,711	$73,711	$73,711	$73,711
Estimated CAM Charges	$8,399	$8,399	$8,399	$8,399	$8,399	$8,399
Miscellaneous Income	-	-	-	-	-	-
TOTAL INCOME	$82,110	$82,110	$82,110	$82,110	$82,110	$82,110
EXPENSES						
DIRECT EXPENSES						
Repair & Maintenance	$3,885	$3,885	$3,885	$3,885	$3,885	$3,885
Janitorial	$5,000	$5,000	$5,000	$5,000	$5,000	$5,000
Landscaping/Gardening	$1,748	$1,748	$1,748	$1,748	$1,748	$1,748
Management Fees	$2,874	$2,874	$2,874	$2,874	$2,874	$2,874
Security	$106	$106	$106	$106	$106	$106
Utilities	$4,853	$6,978	$6,108	$6,523	$10,688	$11,282
Insurance	-	-	-	-	-	-
Property Taxes	-	-	$39,787	-	-	-
TOTAL DIRECT EXPENSES	$18,466	$20,591	$59,508	$20,136	$24,301	$24,895
GENERAL & ADMINISTRATIVE						
Bank & Lockbox Fees	$500	$500	$500	$500	$500	$500
Miscellaneous Expense	$250	$250	$250	$250	$250	$250
TOTAL G & A EXPENSE	$750	$750	$750	$750	$750	$750
TOTAL EXPENSES	$19,216	$21,341	$60,258	$20,886	$25,051	$25,645
NET OPERATING INCOME	$62,894	$60,769	$21,852	$61,224	$57,059	$56,465
DEBT SERVICE	($23,966)	($23,966)	($23,966)	($23,966)	($23,966)	($23,966)
OWNER DISTRIBUTIONS	($15,938)	($15,938)	($15,938)	($15,938)	($15,938)	($15,938)
CASH FLOW	$22,991	$20,866	($18,051)	$21,321	$17,156	$16,562

Not only do these help you manage your investment and maximize your profits, they double as the reports you send your investors and partners if you have them. If you don't have investors, relax; your work will still be worthwhile because your lenders will want to see these reports, too. In fact, often the loan specifies that you will give the lender reports on a regular basis. They want to make sure you are working your plan and that your plan is effective

Make Arrangements for Ongoing Accounting: This is one of those transitions you will have to make from the former owner to yourself. It can be as simple as transferring his or her QuickBooks file to you or it can be as complicated as building or rebuilding an accounting system for the property. Either way, you'll want to decide whether or not you want to do the accounting yourself. Personally, I have a bookkeeper who does this for me and she is worth her weight in gold. We meet regularly and go over all the numbers. For me, that works best.

WITH ALL THE FACTS IN HAND...

With all the facts in hand, it's time to make the decision to go or not go on this property. So what will it be? Are you officially the owner or are you not? If there was something that raised an important red flag in this process and you are deciding strongly to pass on this property, then here is a tip on how to back out of a deal gracefully. I believe honesty (or as close to honesty as you can get without offending the owner by telling him his building is a disaster) is the best policy because it's all about building relationships.

In most cases, you will move forward, and that means it's time to look at leasing and keeping your building leased.

CHAPTER 12

LEASE IT AND KEEP IT LEASED

I f you build it, they will come. If you own it, they will lease it. No they won't! On both counts. As much as you may like to think that everyone will be as excited about your investment as you are, this simply is not the case. In most markets, there are lots of buildings for rent and lots of choices for business owners regardless of whether the owner is a $500-per-hour law firm looking for a Class A high-rise, a master carpenter looking for multi-use workshop space to create custom furnishings, or anything in-between. Choices abound, as they say.

So what does it take to lease your building and keep it leased? It takes attracting good tenants. It takes professional management that makes the experience of being in your building an exceptional one. It takes understanding the big difference between a leasing company and a management company.

I see so many first-time commercial property owners and even those who should know better think they can lease their properties themselves. While many know they don't want to manage the properties themselves—after all, the thought of the Friday 5:00 pm toilet clog is enough to tame that crazy notion—I'm always surprised when people say they want to do their own leasing. My only conclusion is that they don't realize what is involved. I know from experience if they are not set up for leasing—and most building owners are not—it is nearly impossible to successfully lease a building. Building owners may also rationalize by thinking that there is no reason to pay a commission to an agent when they can do the leasing themselves.

I believe that, right up there with being able to analyze a deal and performing good due diligence, is leasing your property. Why so much importance? Because leasing drives your cash flow. Cash flow is a significant definer of property value. This is so important that my second book is focused entirely on the subject of its title: *The Art of Commercial Real Estate Leasing.*

THE TYPES OF LEASES AVAILABLE

There are four kinds of leases in all. The type of lease that you have for your tenants will dictate the amount of involvement that you and your property managers will have maintaining and paying for upkeep to your properties.

The decision to go with one lease or another depends on the market and what tenants are accustomed to paying in that market. In Chicago or New York, for example, it's triple net for office, and on the West Coast it's gross. Even within a single building, there can be different tenants signed to different types of leases.

Here is a refresher from earlier in this book on the types of leases that are out there. Get to know them. They will become your language as you continue along your path as a real estate professional.

Gross: Gross means full service. You as property owner would pay for all utilities, upkeep and maintenance. The tenant pays for everything in one check to the owner.

Net: This can mean a number of things, but generally it means the tenant pays for one or more aspects of the property's utilities, upkeep, and maintenance. For example, net-utilities means the tenant will pay for utilities. net-janitorial means the tenant will pay for janitorial.

Triple Net: In this type of lease, the owner is responsible for structure, roof, parking, etc., or maintaining capital elements to the building. But the tenant covers all other expenses it takes to operate the building, including utilities, taxes, utility repair, maintenance, etc. Companies like Walgreens®, Jack in the Box®, etc. typically sign triple net leases. Triple net is designated NNN in the industry, and you'll see it often on sales literature.

Absolute Triple Net: Here, the tenant pays everything, real estate taxes, janitorial, and all capital improvements, which includes replacing the roof if it caves in. This is the least amount of work for you, but you'll find these leases are typically in single-tenant buildings where the tenant almost owns the building. They are typically long-term leases and sometimes are what are known as "sale lease back" deals in which a tenant owner sells his or her own building to an investor, then leases it back for a long-term agreement.

LEASING IS MARKETING

The reality is, in most cases, that investors can't lease the building themselves because it takes leasing and communications knowledge that most investors don't have. Leasing is actually marketing, and unless you know this specialty; investors' efforts are trial and mostly error. I am an investor, but I am also a leasing agent/advisor and have been one for more than two decades. I know through my own successes and failures how to effectively lease a building. I know that leasing a building starts with a good marketing plan. You may think that all there is to leasing a building is putting a sign out front and praying, but there's a lot more to it. In fact, when I am working with a client, we develop an entire marketing plan that is designed to generate awareness of the building and interest in its features and benefits.

Our basic approach is two-pronged. First, we go business-to-consumer, meaning we market directly to those persons or companies that may be in a position to lease. Second, we go business-to-business within our trade so that every other leasing agent/advisor is aware of the property, its particulars, and its availabilities. A good leasing agent/advisor knows how to work his or her own industry and knows how to create buzz about a property. He or she knows how to position your property as more lucrative than others to fellow leasing agents/advisors, and how to steer them toward you and away from your competition.

The truth about leasing is that the space always follows the business. By that I mean that business owners look for space that reflects what the business does and how it operates and how it succeeds. A creative advertising business, for example, would not seek out a Plain-Jane, white-walled shell with a sea of built-in cubicles. No, a creative business like that would look for space that is interestingly designed with unexpected hallway angles, unique finishes, and moody lighting. How many of those spaces exist? Not many. That is why so much of leasing is looking at a space for what it can become, not what it is at the moment. It takes a very skilled leasing agent/advisor to have this vision and then be able to communicate it to the client. If the company doesn't see itself in the space, then that's it. No deal.

Funny thing about this business is that every building owner thinks their own space is not only wonderful, but that everyone will want it. They all think that it will lease or sublet very easily because it's so perfect. They are always surprised when no one shares their enthusiasm. But they shouldn't be. The building and the space is a fit for the owner or the existing tenant, but not necessarily a fit for anyone else. It happens all the time, so be prepared to either have a lot of vision or hire someone who does, and who can market the sizzle along with the space.

LEASING IS SELLING

Leasing is marketing, but leasing is selling, too. That's the part that surprises many property owners. I'm not exactly sure why. When I am working with a property owner, the sales and negotiation process is time-consuming and takes experience and expert knowledge of selling and the market. It takes professionals years to discover what works when it comes to positioning the benefits of a product, minimizing the shortcomings, and overcoming objections.

It's also taken me years to get that gut instinct about a prospective tenant. As much as I wish I could teach you that in this chapter, I can't. I can tell you a horror story, however, about a project in my market and an owner who decided to go it alone and lease the rest of his building after the first two floors were leased by a broker. They had found and placed in those spaces excellent businesses that were growing and successful—upstanding, too. The top floor of the building was being saved for one big tenant that had the type of business that would value the exceptional views the nearly floor-to-ceiling windows afforded, and who could handle the pricier rent.

Well, the building owner got a little impatient and a little greedy thinking he could do this himself. "After all," he thought, "leasing doesn't seem that hard. Why should I pay a leasing agent/advisor for something I can do myself?" So he fired his broker. And within no time, the building owner had a tenant. The problem was, the tenant wanted only a portion of the top-floor space. The building owner figured, "What the heck," and leased it. Bad decision. Making that bad decision worse was the fact that the tenant was a medical practice for transgender surgery. Everyone is entitled to his or her own life choices, but let me tell you what happened to the building.

Within a year, the quality business tenants in the lower floors had moved out and on the top floor near the medical practice a hair club for men moved in. It was all downhill from there. In less than a year, a solid Class A property with a quality tenant mix became an undesirable property to all but a few fringe businesses. Quite a shame.

Professional leasing agents/advisors know what can happen if you lease to the wrong kinds of tenants. Little did this guy know we turned down the businesses that he naively signed. You get what you pay for.

In my experience, the best leasing folks are the ones who know how to provide the vision that the client wants to hear. They don't do this out of thin air or try to stuff ten pounds of potatoes into a five-pound bag. They do it by knowing the client and understanding the needs and the business. They have a feel for the kind of space that will really excite. The best leasing people know how to create a match between client and space, and then have the ability to sell the vision, even if it is not completely obvious.

The vision is more than just how the space looks—or can look—on the inside. There are many more variables, which we will get to shortly. Many of them are just as, if not more, important than the interior space itself. No building is perfect, but it is the job of the leasing agent/advisor to assemble the top picks, inspire them, and close the deal.

LEASING IS DETAIL WORK

Leasing a building is seldom easy; actually, it is quite the opposite. That's becoming obvious. It's generally very labor intensive. When we're doing a marketing plan for a building, we begin by looking at the property and effectively positioning it in the market. That requires us to do an intense market study of all competing properties—both the ones that are already there and the ones expected to be completed in the coming months or year. By understanding the market, we can find the gaps that will make the property we're representing far more desirable and therefore more leasable.

Our work doesn't stop there. We look at all the comparables and analyze each deal to understand the specifics and find the clues we need for our own success. We even look at the transaction activity rate within the vicinity of the property we are representing to see any trends up, down, or sideways. We don't stop until we have a full picture of the market. From these details we formulate the true value of a building or a space, and that enables us to set the rental prices and all the terms that accompany a lease. This includes operating expenses, tenant improvements, free rent, other concessions, parking terms, security deposits—I could go on and on. It's pretty extensive.

So often, I see people who are doing their own leasing price a space out of the market. The first reason they do it is, as you recall, their space "is perfect and everyone will want it." Right? Wrong. We know that argument doesn't hold any credence. The other reason is, they have not done their homework or they have done it poorly. Often, they are comparing their building or space to space of a higher quality or class. The final reason they overprice is because they are setting the price based on how much they paid for the building itself. How much you pay for a building has nothing to do with how much you can charge tenants for rent. An important lesson of leasing: the market sets the rental prices, not you.

As with any good sales function, eventually prospecting begins. From lists and sources that we have developed over time and others that we would develop specifically for the project at hand, we send our literature and make cold calls to gauge interest. We work inside and outside the target location; we even do out-of-state prospecting, targeting companies that are coming into town. We give a lot of presentations to tenants in other properties that are in our target size and business range.

As I mentioned earlier, we'll also work within our industry and communicate regularly with the other agents/advisors community. We identify which ones specialize in buildings like the one we are representing. We do our presentations to their offices and their staff. We use email and direct mail and we host parties, etc. to keep others informed about the properties we represent.

Of course, we use the sophistication of the Internet to help us target those business prospects who are using the Web to troll for new office space. Our sophisticated websites are searchable and detailed. We are connected directly to listing services and our user interface is the result of more than ten years of improvements. Clearly, you're beginning to see that a lot goes into finding the right tenants and getting a lease signed sooner rather than later.

Once we understand how we're going to market the property and to which companies, we create a development strategy that will outline our plans to fill the building. This is a complete plan that includes rent rates, leasing terms, expense stops (the maximum expenses per square foot for the building), tenant improvement limits, other concessions, even commissions.

The sign in front of the building may be the most visible part, but it is the smallest part of the marketing efforts for a building. If only it was as easy as hammering a sign into the ground and answering the phone. The truth is, experience is everything in the process. There are literally an unlimited number of pits that the novice can fall into. Over the course of our careers, we have fallen into them all. That's another reason leasing agents/advisors are so valuable—they've already taken the falls for you.

THE DEAL MAKERS AND DEAL BREAKERS IN LEASING

Earlier in this chapter, I mentioned that it takes more than the vision of great space (meaning space that matches the business) to actually get the business. There are more variables that come into play. I believe there are numerous variables that every client will consider before signing on the dotted line. Here's my top-twenty list:

1. Rates: Of course, every client is going to be concerned with the rent and the cost per square foot because almost every client has a budget. They know how much their business can allocate to this expense line item. I work to stay within my clients' budgets, not trying to oversell them. It is in everyone's best interest to have a client that pays on time every month. Rental rate is one of the most important considerations on the list.

2. **Term:** The length of the lease agreement is another important factor. Sometimes my user clients are looking for a short-term fix and sometimes they want the lease agreement to run longer in exchange for some other consideration. This can be a highly negotiable variable, and the match is made when the term connects with the client's objectives.

3. **Free Rent:** Many building owners offer free rent for some length of time as part of the negotiated agreement. Aspects to be considered are the number of months and what is included. Is it just the rent, or does it cover common area maintenance fees, parking fees, etc.?

4. **Tenant Improvements:** Many lease agreements have negotiated into them some allowance money for tenant improvements, or TIs. This can be a lot of money or a little money. A good leasing agent/advisor will know the current market and know what a realistic yet generous amount to request is. A rookie can really mess up an otherwise good deal by demanding too much, or cause a client to overpay by not asking for enough.

5. **Layout:** This refers to the interior floor plan, the shape and size of the space. Sometimes, square or rectangular spaces are a plus; at other times, oddly shaped space is what a client is looking for. It all depends on the client and the business. Again, when I know a client's objectives, I know what space configurations will work and what ones won't.

6. **Quality of Building:** The building exterior on a commercial property is like the curb appeal on a residential property. It says a lot about your business just as a home says a lot about you. A prestigious building with excellent upkeep and landscaping says to the world that this company is a player, that it is reputable and can handle my business. A shoddy-looking building tells the world that a company might be fly-by-night, not very progressive, or just plain cheap. If "the clothes make the man," as the saying goes, the building exterior makes the business.

7. Parking Type and Ratio: I've walked away from buildings as an investor and as a leasing advisor because the property is under-parked; in other words, the number of parking spaces for the size of the building is light. I know my client's customers will not be happy if, every time they visit, they have to allot an extra ten minutes to search for a place to park. Nothing is worse than a building that doesn't have enough parking, and in most cases there is little that can be done about it.

8. Parking Location: As bad as it is to not have enough parking spaces, clients also don't like having to park far away from a building. The reasons are obvious, with safety concerns being one of the biggest. No one likes the idea of walking a distance through a dark parking lot or alleyway to get to the car. And it's no fun to walk a distance—briefcase, workout bag, coffee cup, and cell phone in hand—to get into the building in the morning. We won't even talk about rain, snow, and ice. Parking should be easy and safe.

9. Efficiency: Clients look for generally efficient buildings, meaning ones that are easy to find, get into, walk through, locate the businesses, find the restrooms, etc. Some buildings—and you probably can think of a few yourself—are just plain poorly designed. It's hard to find the entry, it's hard to find the elevator, it's hard to find the office numbers, it's hard to get to the restrooms, and the list goes on.

10. Access: Here's a big one. Accessibility refers to how easy it is to get into and out of the building site. Some buildings have excellent access and others do not. I just moved one company because the business owner hated making an unprotected left-hand turn across a very busy street every time he turned into the building. While we were looking for his new space, he would joke that he was going to hold me personally responsible if he got into a wreck while he impatiently waited! We found him space with better access, and he is much happier.

11. **Signage:** Some businesses need very visible signage and others do not. This is one of the negotiation points that is critical for businesses that rely on either walk-in business or that want to use their building signage as awareness advertising.

12. **Amenities On-Site:** Some buildings have shopping, banking, places to eat, dry cleaners, and more perks right on-site in lobbies or in underground retail centers. To some of our clients, these conveniences matter. I know one person who leases in a building on a small municipal airport runway that has hangar space for corporate jets. That's a big amenity for some business owners.

13. **Amenities Off-Site:** Then there are some buildings that seem to be on an island all their own. There's no place to go for lunch, there's no grocery store nearby, there's little to nothing around. Sometimes this is the nature of new development—retail and restaurants have not moved in yet—but sometimes it's just the way it is.

14. **Property Management:** Good property management is like a gourmet meal that has great presentation, tastes amazing, and completely satisfies you. And best of all, you never have to be concerned with any of the details. It's just there for you to enjoy. Bad property management lets you know it's there at every turn. To go back to our gourmet meal, you have to ask for the salt, your silverware isn't clean, the food looks overcooked, and in general, the whole experience is unpleasant. All you see are the details— the missed details.

15. **Ownership:** The ownership matters as much as the property management. Some owners can be terrific landlords and others have baggage. One friend of mine leases space in a building advised by our company. The building owner is a very successful entrepreneur who makes his rounds every so often to his tenant businesses just to see how things are going and to catch up. He's a good guy, a welcomed visitor, and a friend to those who lease from him. There's another building owner down the street who jets off for Cabo every other week and is incredibly unresponsive.

16. **Americans with Disabilities Act Compliance:** To many businesses, this is a very important consideration. It is critical that those who use wheelchairs have easy and safe access to all areas of the building and grounds.

17. **Location, Location, Location:** Some space has views of beautiful vistas and other space has no view at all. Some space is visible right off the elevator and other space is tucked back in some insignificant hallway corner. The location within the building matters. It says a lot about a business.

18, 19, and 20. **Location of the Building Itself:** This is most critical requirement and that's why it is not just number 18 on our list, but 19 and 20, too. The right location is one of the absolute musts.

WHAT TO LOOK FOR IN A LEASING AGENT/ ADVISOR

My hope is, with the stories and the workload described in this chapter so far, I've convinced you to at least consider the value of having a leasing agent/advisor working on your side. If that's the case, then I should also point out that not all leasing agents/advisors are created equal. There are leasing agents out there who don't do their homework and say "yes" to shaky businesses all the time. There are leasing agents who don't know the market, leasing agents who are terrible negotiators, and leasing agents who simply can't sell. If you're going to hire a leasing agent—and I suggest you do—hire a good one, a true advisor. Aside from the obvious qualities like experience, motivation, organization, intelligence, expertise, and integrity, here's what else to look for:

Relationship vs. Transaction: Although real estate seems like a huge industry, it really is a small, local industry. Each city or town has a small, tightly knit, and much-intertwined real estate community. It is critical to find a leasing broker/advisor who sees his or her job as one of relationship building, not just completing transactions. I have spent the last twenty years doing deals, and in the process, have built excellent relationships with the real estate professionals where I live and work. This effort pays off for me and my clients every day.

The reality is, most transactions happen through other leasing agents/advisors. The opportunities come in through them and we market our owners' opportunities outbound through them. How eager would they be to bring to me top-quality tenants or even be interested in looking at space I pitch to them if I had a reputation for win-lose arrangements where I win and they lose? Not very.

As a rule, I put a great deal of time and energy into providing lots of information to prospects and clients. Even if there is no agreement for representation, I generally am eager to help because I know that's how to build a relationship. Experience has proven to me that relationships eventually pay off. One experience I recall was when a large healthcare insurance provider was moving into town. A high-powered agent came in from New York and called our office and said she was coming in to look at space. I asked if she needed local representation, and she said no. Regardless, I told her I'd get her a list of available buildings by the next day.

We met and, during that meeting, I helped her in every way that I could. When she returned to New York, she told her boss she had met an agent who could really help and that she wanted to work with. He said no, but she insisted. Long story short, she got her way, and I ended up doing not one but nearly fifty transactions with that company. Had I not been willing to freely give of my time and knowledge, I would not have been on the receiving end of that lucrative piece of business.

Rapport with You: This whole leasing effort has to be a partnership. There has to be a good rapport. A good leasing agent/advisor understands your objectives, and then works to match the right space and the right tenants. Plus, a good leasing agent/advisor willingly takes on even small businesses or buildings and educates them as they grow into bigger businesses. I found space for one software company many years ago. It was the company's first space when it was just three people strong. I think the office was all of 1,200 square feet. At the time, I was doing much bigger deals, but to me that didn't matter. We developed rapport, and within a few years, I handled the transactions surrounding the company's 137,000 square foot corporate office and more than 44 offices worldwide. It happens.

Location Knowledge: Any leasing agent/advisor you work with must have not only a general knowledge of the metro area, but also intimate knowledge of the submarket area where your building is located. This comes back to the fact that real estate is really a small, localized industry. The best leasing agents/advisors are the ones most knowledgeable—not about the whole city or town—but about one square mile. Find this person and you'll be in good shape. It's not hard; just drive around and look at whose name appears on the leasing signs most frequently.

Deal Maker vs. Processor: There are leasing agents out there who are not advisors. They are the people who do little more than play middleman and shuttle messages back and forth between prospect and building owner. That's not the type of representation you want. You want an agent/advisor who will add value by working for you and negotiating on your behalf. Anyone who has some training can relay information and process paper, but that's not what you are paying for. You want to find a true advisor who can weed out the ridiculous and the no-chance-in-you-know-where offers and deal points to get to the end game quickly and efficiently.

Reputation: Finally, and this probably goes without saying, you want a leasing agent/advisor with a solid reputation in the community. How can you be sure? You ask around. You talk to other building owners and talk to other business owners who have worked with the person you are considering. It's worth the extra time and the effort to do this and can be the first step to developing a leasing agent/advisor partner for life.

These are the qualities I have developed in myself over the years, and they are the same qualities that I work to foster in young people who are entering this profession. Not all can cut it. The requirements are demanding. And if they can't cut it, they either get out of the business altogether or move over to my competition. Either is okay with me.

Choosing your leasing agent/advisor partner is one of the most important decisions you will ever make. It can mean the difference between a property that generates positive cash flow and one that doesn't. It can mean the difference between owning an asset or a liability. A good leasing agent/advisor can actually enhance the reputation and standing of your business within the community and bring you more business along with more profitability.

CHAPTER 12

THE LAST WORD...

COPPOLA'S 5 RULES OF LEASING

1. I will not need every deal.

2. I will discuss challenges with the client immediately.

3. I will not allow a commission to drive any transaction.

4. I will consider long-term relationships more important than any fee.

5. I will develop a professionalism that provides me access to all decision makers.

CHAPTER 13

NOW THAT YOU'RE AN INVESTOR

Congratulations for making it to this point in the process. Whether you have actually put any of your own money on the line yet or not, you now know what it takes to succeed in the world of commercial real estate. You have learned it takes establishing your goals, narrowing your focus, understanding the terminology, learning everything you can, becoming a market and sub-market expert, finding the opportunities, eliminating the distractions, choosing the winning property, drafting and signing a letter of intent, performing your due diligence, and, finally—if all the indicators point to go—sign the deal.

That's a long to-do list, and each item on it packs hours of work behind it. But my guess is by now, you actually enjoy the work you just performed, you have a deep motivation to become a commercial real estate investor, and your motivation hasn't wavered since you learned exactly what that job entails. So what is your motivation now? Is it different from what you thought it would be when you started on page one?

Many people know they want to be rich, whether they use that term or not. Some say they want to be comfortable. Others say they want no financial worries. In a way, they all mean the same thing. It means people don't want to be poor, and that's fully understandable. But when being rich, comfortable, or without financial worries takes hard work, it makes those without conviction ask themselves if it is worth it. That's a valid question.

Some will answer that question quickly by saying they are real estate investors for the financial returns it provides. They want and enjoy the passive cash flow. The thought of making money while sleeping is compelling. That's their view until they realize that a lot of work is involved during the waking hours, particularly in the beginning. Then they ask, "Is it worth it?"

Thinking back, if my pursuit of investing in real estate started with my pursuit for money—for money's sake—it didn't last long. It quickly moved to the pursuit of my future and the freedom I wanted to have in the years to come. I saw commercial real estate as a pathway to the things I wanted in life. The money quickly became the currency I needed to create my future and the measure of my success.

In my years as an investor and a commercial broker/advisor, I have taken bets on many young people who wanted to break into this business and hired them. They usually come in highly motivated and charged about the financial prospects. I can usually tell within a week whether they have the underlying motivation to stick with this business. I can tell by their willingness to learn, by the hours they keep, by their ability to sacrifice some things today for freedom tomorrow. That last one is tough. You have to have some pretty big dreams and powerful motivation to overcome that one. We live, as you know, in a society based on instant gratification.

Real estate is not about instant gratification. It is a way of life— life in which, if you do things consistently right, there's a good chance for a big pay-off later. When I think about it, I'm actually glad real estate isn't about instant gratification. If it were, the business would be full of the people I usually end up firing—the people who don't want to work hard today for something bigger and better tomorrow.

In real estate, I meet tremendous people all the time and learn something from them at every turn. They are the people who know how to break through the barriers and succeed when others quit.

People with perseverance end up doing more things, and doing those things well. I shudder to think what our office buildings, homes, stadiums, and every other place where we live, laugh, work, and enjoy life would be like if it were up to the people in our society who want everything now without the effort. It takes toughness to pursue excellence and get close to achieving it.

Don't get me wrong; I hope you are so excited about your investments and your new-found passion that you are jumping out of your shoes to find that first or that next deal. You see, there's a difference between just wanting the winnings and enjoying the game. This business takes both, with a very heavy dose of the latter. If you don't enjoy the game, you likely won't get the winnings.

The game for me is the challenge of creating value in real estate. It's a game of strategy, endurance, and speed all in one. There's a little hide-and-seek mixed in, too. Looking under rocks and turning up that opportunity everyone else missed is an amazing feeling. It's confidence building and a win in its own right. Just when I think I've got it all down, that I know how the game works, the field changes, the market shifts, and the learning begins again.

When I began this book, I spoke about my professional accomplishments and said the one that means the most to me is the photo of my first deal. That first deal was and is everything. It changed me forever. Real estate value comes in that form, too.

You, too, will have a first deal. You will have a life-changing beginning. Look beyond the dollars for the value within. That will help you persevere through the ups and the downs, and you will find value takes on more shapes than you can ever imagine and that you may not even recognize for years to come. Happy hunting and happy succeeding.

ABOUT THE AUTHOR

R. Craig Coppola is the top producing office broker in Lee & Associates' 35 year history, as well as one of the Founding Principals of Lee & Associates Arizona. He has completed over 3,500 lease and sale transactions over the past 30 years, totaling a value in excess of $3,500,000,000. Craig is among the very few—less than 40 worldwide—who has earned the top three designations in the real estate industry: CCIM, CRE and SIOR.

How to Win in Commercial Real Estate is Craig's first book and his second, *The Art of Commercial Real Estate Leasing*, is scheduled to publish in the fall of 2014.

Craig served as NAIOP Chapter President of the Year in 2003, the highest personal honor given by the largest real estate development trade association (National Association of Industrial and Office Properties). In addition, he has been awarded NAIOP's office broker of the year six times. Craig is also a Past Chairman of the Southwest Chapter of CRE (Counselors of Real Estate). CRE is a trade organization representing the finest real estate consultants for over 50 years.

A third generation Arizonan and father of four remarkable children, Craig holds a Bachelor's Degree in Finance from Nicholls State University and a Master's Degree in Business Administration from Arizona State University. He and his wife are active within the Phoenix community and Craig is a sought-after national speaker on real estate and motivational topics.

Index